Autumn 1995

five

Printed in the Czech Republic

Trafika is published by Trafika Press Inc., a not-for-profit corporation in the State of New York. **Trafika** is published in part with public funds from the US National Endowment for the Arts.

Post Office Box 250413
New York, NY 10025-1536
USA

Veverkova 20
170 00 Prague 7
the Czech Republic

ISSN 1210-6488
ISBN 1-885304-04-8

Distributors
Fine Print Distribution, Austin, TX; Ingram Periodicals, La Vergne, TN; Ubiquity Distributors, Brooklyn, NY; Small Press Distributors, Berkeley, CA; Marginal Distributors, Peterborough, ONT; Turnaround Distribution, London

Subscription Services
EBSCO, Faxon, Readmore, Harrassowitz, SWETS

Subscriptions
Individuals: $35/£25; Institutions: $40/£28
AMEX, VISA, or check/money order payable to:
Trafika Press Inc., NY

Typeset in Bembo, Frutiger, Meta
Lithography by Proxima
Printed by Tiskarna HUGO, Prague

In Memoriam
Lukáš Tomin (1963 – 1995)

Trafika No 5
Autumn 1995

ZAFER *Şenocak*

The Man in the Undershirt

At five I learned my first prayer by heart. A short prayer: Kulhuvallahuahadallahussamedlamyalidvalamyuledvallamyakunlahu-kufuvenahad. That means: He is the one God, the eternal God, He does not beget and is not begotten, and no one is His equal. I didn't know how you begot. You spoke a prayer as you bowed down, sat in an uncomfortable position on the floor, sensing your weight on your toes, and touched the floor with your forehead.

At six I touched the floor with my forehead. My father showed me a dark spot on his forehead and said, "This spot will not burn in hell." "But you're not going to hell," I answered. "One never knows," said Father. I thought about how you could pray to have as many such marks as possible on your body. But there was only one proper posture for prayer.

At seven I prayed with many other people. It was loud and dusty and smelled like sweat. I read *Robinson Crusoe* and wondered how this man had held out all alone on an island without dying.

At eight I met people who never prayed. At nine, people who prayed totally differently from us. They sat on hard benches or just kneeled, instead of prostrating themselves. "Those are proud people," said Father. "And God will punish them for that. Besides, they attribute a son to God, God, who has never begotten."

I still didn't know how you begot.

I sat with the people God would punish in their houses of prayer. It was cold and dark. I didn't move from my spot. My teacher sat next to me. I asked her how you beget. She acted like she didn't understand my question. I didn't dare ask again. I asked a different way: "Why does God have a son?" "God loves men so much that He created them, and to show His love, He came to them in the form of a man." "But God will also punish, namely those who say He has a son," I answered, convinced, and my teacher smiled. After that I never went to Christian services again.

At twelve I learned to read the Koran. A foreign script, foreign words. Reading without understanding is a strange experience; it's as if you touch a figure that isn't there. I started to pray regularly, and gradually began to understand what begetting meant. It was nice. And God renounced doing such a nice thing? God was a strange figure. I loved Him, but I didn't understand Him.

At fourteen my father picked me up from a class party because it was 7:30 at night. He knew as well as I did that begetting happens after 7:30, and what God didn't grant himself certainly wasn't right for a boy like me.

At fifteen I noticed that even more incomprehensible but also nicer things preceded begetting. The reason for these realizations was a girl. Everything on her body was light.

At sixteen I gave up praying regularly and secretly broke my fast. I didn't have any pangs of conscience.

At seventeen I got stomach pains and had the measles. I discussed the meaning and purpose of belief with my father. We discussed hunger, need, and misery. I read evil things and thought: When evil is written down, it is no longer evil. I myself started to write evil things. One of the texts was called "The Adventure of a Tree under an Ax." It was fifteen lines long. I always counted the lines when I was finished and wondered about writers who could write thick books.

At seventeen I discovered Kafka and forgot everything that I had read before. I fell unhappily in love for the next five years. I went for long walks in the forest with my unhappy love. I had to write. It was great fun to write. After each text I had an indescribably happy feeling. When I tried to describe this happiness, words failed me. I ate pork for the first time. It didn't taste like the devil. So many important things happened to me at seventeen.

At eighteen I drank wine. It was during my first trip through Italy, in Florence. If I hadn't drunk wine there I would have had the feeling I had never even been there. I smoked. I smoked a lot. At night I hardly slept. I moved out of the house and into a small room behind an office with tiny windows at eye level which looked into a garage.

I lived there with my books. At nineteen, I loved a girl there for the first time. It was a short but very intense affair. For three weeks you dream of a shared future, of many children, you exchange sour-tasting juices like mad, you are jealous, you tremble all over, and then you break up on an outing to a lake near the city as if there had never been anything between you.

At twenty-two I published my first book of poems. Twenty poems which had to do with all kinds of evil, above all with the city and its civilized trash chutes. I had seen *One Hundred Twenty Days of Sodom* at the movies. I went to the movies almost every night. The movies supplanted reading. I wanted to write the way other people made movies. A man fell in love with me. I didn't feel anything toward him and took refuge in women I hardly knew. This row of women formed a dark canal from which there was no escape. I heard and read about a new disease that could catch you in the canal.

At twenty-five I translated the poems of an Anatolian mystic from the 14th century. My father accompanied me through his language. He now had a gray beard. His belief was a rock that he carried on his back without allowing anyone to notice his burden. If Camus had known him he would have rewritten his *Myth of Sisyphus*. I read the Koran in German translation for the first time. I understood Goethe, who said that this book disgusts and demands respect at the same time. I believed as much as ever in Him, but had forgotten His name. His unproven graciousness consoled me. He was cruel, but He was also the only being you could impute graciousness to, despite His cruelty. Others went into armed battle for Him. Either you loved for Him or you killed for Him. Both were convincing. A woman bound me to her for good by being with me without making herself noticeable. Our relationship was silent and stable. Without results. I wrote to keep from thinking. I wrote out of pain, to keep from feeling the pain.

At thirty I read in Salman Rushdie: "What is the opposite of faith? Not disbelief. Too final, certain, closed. Itself a kind of belief. Doubt."

10 We have new neighbors. For several weeks now. They moved into the apartment on the ground floor, the one that you have to pass to enter the building, through the remarkably big old front door with the broken panes that's open at all hours. You push the door open and go up three steps, and you can see for yourself the green-painted door in the dark on the left. Provided you don't let yourself get too distracted by the scrawls along the staircase, where lately two rival gangs have been conducting linguistic

duels. The nameplate next to the doorbell dangling loosely from its wires is blank. But whenever you come, you always hear noises in the apartment. Is someone making a phone call? Does this apartment, which stood empty for months after the last old lady in the building lived and died of old age there, even have a telephone? The old lady was so hard of hearing that from afternoon to night her television supplied the whole building with noises – barely understandable news moderators, bits of sound like music, the rhythmic clapping of talk show audiences.

Sometimes noises can be like sponges, absorbing loneliness. Ever since the television from the ground floor has been silent, loneliness has swollen behind many doors. The apartments where people live alone become cramped, which I know from my own apartment on the second floor above the new neighbors.

Three men are there. Three lean foreign-looking dark-skinned men. Men amplify the foreignness felt toward them. It's as if they make every distance greater. While exotic-looking women almost provoke nearness, an incomprehensible speechless nearness of flesh and tongues, accepted by each person without question.

"Dubious figures," says Michaela, the neighbor who lives across from me. "Besides, they speak the language that I want to forget." Until her naturalization, Michaela was named Melike. Now she teaches German to immigrants. Anyone who quarrels with his own German identity is just fine by her. Before she started going to night school to get her high school diploma, Michaela, alias Melike, was a hairdresser, or, more precisely, an apprentice in a salon in the neighborhood, not far from the house where she was born. She lived with her parents, who were proud of their pretty and always well-dressed daughter. They even allowed her to paint her fingernails bright red. They hoped for a good catch. Melike dreamed of a bank employee and regularly read fashion magazines. Michaela's parents were relatively liberal and allowed their daughter the right to dream. "He just can't be German," her father used to say. "But he can have himself circumcised," Melike had responded once. It was the one and only time in her life her father ever slapped her. A loud slap that left marks, not just a burning red cheek.

Melike broke off her apprenticeship, moved from her parents' house here to Donaustraße. The fact that she only moved a few hundred meters away, without changing neighborhoods, in breathing and seeing range of her parents, relatives, and acquaintances, was an enormous provocation. She was the first to move out, to quit her apprenticeship, to go back to get a high school degree, to be left by a German boyfriend, and to leave two German boyfriends who had fallen fatally in love with her, out of revenge. She started to study. Then she took German citizenship and changed her name.

Maybe that was why it took so long for a friendship to be able to develop with my neighbor, although we always had lively and long discussions when we met each other, even when we were in a hurry. But a Michaela who had earlier been called Melike repelled me. It was as if I was looking into a wound, into half a face, when I saw into her very striking almond eyes and the strongly expressive mouth, which gave her somewhat unapproachable beauty an exotic tone. When a Turk takes German citizenship he doesn't become a German to me, even if he has to give up his Turkish passport. But what does a Melike become, when she's called Michaela after taking on German citizenship? A super-German, an unbearable identity? Or a malicious undermining of German identity? That kind of person can only have enemies, I thought, and it was hard for me to deal with our friendship or even to admit the attraction I felt toward her.

But now, since the three dubious characters moved in downstairs, everything's been different. I sense that I will soon have to decide how near I want to be to Michaela. Not only that, but Hanna, the woman I've been intimate with for many years (that's what I call all of my exes), left me during the night and on a spontaneous whim took off for a bike trip through Tadzhikistan. To a country where, as she said, men are busy making war and therefore have no time to bother foreign women. I'm not so sure that will be the case when they see their first woman on a bicycle, I think, gloating, of course without saying anything about it to her. The stupid cow will see where she stands without the unstable men around her whose whining she has had enough of. We'll see how long she holds out with her heroes.

I nod to everything. That binds me to my generation. Smiling and nodding. But where is the hate? Who or what do we hate, someone in me wants to know. Piercing questions from an eternal companion who always ambushes me at the wrong time, most recently during intercourse. Long painful cramps in my left leg. The girl advises me to have myself tested for AIDS. Then this pitying look, which could have made me impotent forever.

The lukewarm night. The surrounding houses whisper peculiarly. How foreign this city is suddenly. How different its familiar smell. Hanna is missing. And the three dark characters argue loudly as I go by their door. What do I know about why they live there and why they're dark? I still haven't spoken a word with them, but I know one of them vaguely. He once lived in the corner building on Sonnenallee until it was ripped down. Then he disappeared for years. Everyone who lived there has more or less disappeared. Advanced junkies and a few unemployed bachelors who were going on sixty. They lived together in a communal apartment under the roof and sometimes threw empty beer bottles out the window. The one that I know vaguely – maybe he just seems familiar to me – smuggled the others into the country. Smuggling is his business. But since the city's no longer an island, smugglers have a hard time of it. Since the city's open on all sides again, everybody thinks he has a claim to it. The secret languages disappear. The secret tips are offered in tourist books, and informers show their faces. The sanitation department is overwhelmed. Everyone lays importance in a white collar, an unstained shirt. Smugglers go under. Just at such a disadvantageous time these curious neighbors show up. They're dark because they all come from the same province. Everyone from that province is dark. There's nothing that can be done about it. There's no prospect for change. Never. The people from those parts are obstinate and reckless. Risk-takers, suited to decide battles and to flounder in normal life. They come from a place I'm not from, where, being more prone to flu and rheumatism, I wouldn't even survive, where I have not been even once in my thirty-five-year-old life. There not only the people's skin but also their business is dark. Doesn't every suspicion begin with dark skin? With the dark skin that cannot be washed off, cannot be covered up? Only whites live on the top floors. The higher one climbs, the whiter they become. An albino couple lives under the roof, they get horribly excited about the cars parked on the sidewalk. Twice they complained about the old woman from the ground floor because of the television, which is too loud, although they live so far up that they could only have known about the noise through hearsay.

Below them lives Barbara the Purified, who no longer hooks on Potsdamer since the Wall opened. She used the early bird's advantage to open a boutique specific to the profession in Prenzlauer Berg. "These days you have to specialize," is her favorite sentence. Whores throughout the city shop at her place, as well as recently a few ladies from Grunewald who have been in town for a short time and so are curious about everything new and surprising. In Berlin everything has changed, they say, although they don't really know how it used to be. Those who have just arrived in town still have a chance to let themselves be carried along by the current of changes, endure unabashedly even the nastiest of surprises. The others, who have already been in town for awhile, imprisoned in their habitual ways, have a bad conscience because of their weariness.

This here is an orderly building, don't let yourself be fooled by the crumbling plaster. The rooms have stuccoed ceilings. The constant onion smell in the hallway? Yes, don't you see that there is a restaurant in the neighboring building whose trash is regularly piled up in our courtyard? It's not the worst place in the neighborhood if you want to eat Indonesian. In your guide it's still under *Indian Restaurants*. The owner changes frequently, you must know. That doesn't necessarily mean anything, does it? Anyway the people in this house all have a clean record, and building management is quite alright. Every year, almost at the same time as the annual heating bills, which they always complete to our benefit because the heater doesn't work most of the winter, they draft a renovation plan, but it regularly flounders due to the landlord, who's never been seen around here. Even so, he's just as stubborn as he is stingy. The rumor's going around that he wants to gradually sell off the apartments in the building. Every time someone moves out or dies everyone expects him to sell. So that the ground floor is already in the hands of speculators. Maybe it's changed owners yet again. In summer the sumptuous old buildings in the neighborhood disappear behind the foliage of the linden and chestnut trees that hem the streets everywhere, you can still get an idea of their size, but their decay can no longer be seen. Only the smell of mold now and then betrays their true condition. But the staircase is regularly cleaned. There's nothing to complain about. Somehow Michaela knows that the three new neighbors are brothers. "Each of them is following a dream," she says. "And not one of them has a real job. They belong to the kind of people who carry heroin with them like a passport – and soon plutonium too." When she talks about the brothers, she almost always lowers her voice, as if their ears were in the walls. "They hire children for a few marks," she says. "To keep a lookout. It's normal where they're from." We argue about the name of the province, where neither of us has been and whose people we know so much about, or I should better say, suspect. But who would presume to draw the exact border between knowledge and suspicion?

"And their dreams?" I ask curiously. "What are their dreams?" "Asses," she says. "Excuse me?" "They want to breed asses." "Here in Berlin? What for?" "Because of the meat. They dream of a sausage factory." The business of the dark-skinned is the dreams of the whites and vice versa, I think to myself. Fantasy is a wind-shielded port for unpaid promissory notes, issued after the death of the dreamer. But not even the costliest renovation will change the hierarchy of color in our building.

I step into the garden in which snails used to house under high trees. I carry the old world on graph paper in my head. Everything new is made of stone and at the same time old, because it's all unchangeable. The stones feed on trees and people.

A tall building, painted green, is outlined against the sky. The laundry which hangs from balconies here and there is the only sign of life.

I go into the building. I feel like I'm blind to the present. Everything new is a nightmare of past things. Or is the old, the past, an image in which the new is mirrored, in ever murkier waters? A world conserved in cellars, which sinks from day to day deeper into the ground, branches out down there, and blooms with new splendor.

The staircase is clean. Fly-free. It smells like cleaning fluid and fresh linoleum. I'm surprised when I notice that there is an elevator. I climb the stairs slowly, as if in this way I could somehow gain time to adjust to the newness. The olive-green plastic door handles are trimmed with brass. On every floor there is a pail with flowers that get light from a hatch in the roof.

Strips of memory stir. They seem grotesque, ornaments in an emphatically neutral surrounding. Which part of memory does that old Ottoman house that once stood here occupy? What has happened to the circular staircase which crept from the hallway up to the third floor? Where are the small towers under the roof? And the balconies, the shutters of carved wood, wood that exuded a particular smell in the heat of summer, which enlivened plants and animals and almost made you forget the water shortage?

Where are they now, those who moved out of this house, out of this city, who smuggled their own lives out in exchange for a worthwhile life somewhere else, outside of their own world? It had become unbearable, and everyone's mind always wanted to escape. It set the route. A route of flames. At night, the mind rummaged through its collected experiences, forged its dreams into plans which seemed almost real, possible. In their dreams they met life unadorned, as well as the plans to escape from life. The real question was whether they would succeed as a group, whether what each regarded as right and possible could also be achieved collectively, or whether some or all of them would remain behind.

An apple that has been ripped off the branch, rotting on the ground, and trampled-on cherries. A pool of blood. Someone dunks his finger in and then plays with a candle, dabs the blood on the shaft, in the flame. Blood doesn't burn.

Someone gives out questionnaires:

Register yourself and don't conceal your plans. Hair color? Eye color? Face shape? How much cash do you have with you? What is the purpose of your stay?

Undoubtedly, they have the right to know everything. Including that which none of us knows, which we will never

performed a dance on the walls of the den, dove into the paintings of the first Turkish painter, played with the colors of the miniatures and the calligraphies. Everything in a frenzy, like insects on an evening in autumn.

Grandfather compared the unfinished poem to wine which had to be stored to mature. From time to time he went into the storeroom and tried, spoke with his animals.

The light goes to my head. I ring at the top, sixth floor, but no one opens. But I should have heard voices in the apartment. Wordless voices. Faltering calls. Faint animal noises.

No window in the light shaft. Only the roof hatch that the spring sun drips through. Why am I sweating? Is it already so hot in April? I pass my moist fingers over the wall. Fresh oil paint. The smell is more intense than on the floors below. I feel that I'm about to catch someone in the act.

On the day that the centuries-old plane tree in the garden was sawed down to make room for the new building, people died on the streets again from the bullets of dissenters.

And Grandfather? His glasses had suddenly disappeared. In the eyes of many, that was the most significant detail that accompanied his death, because he had decreed in his will that they should be laid in the grave with him.

His notebooks, though, he bequeathed to me.

I reach into my jacket pocket and pull out his last notebook. A cheap well-thumbed school notebook, yellowed along the edges, with a small color photo on the cover. The colors are dirty, blurry. An old plane tree, beneath it a couple of rickety tables and chairs. The people in the chairs hardly recognizable anymore.

I open the notebook and start to write.

Translated from German by Nancy Isenson

Javier *MARÍAS*

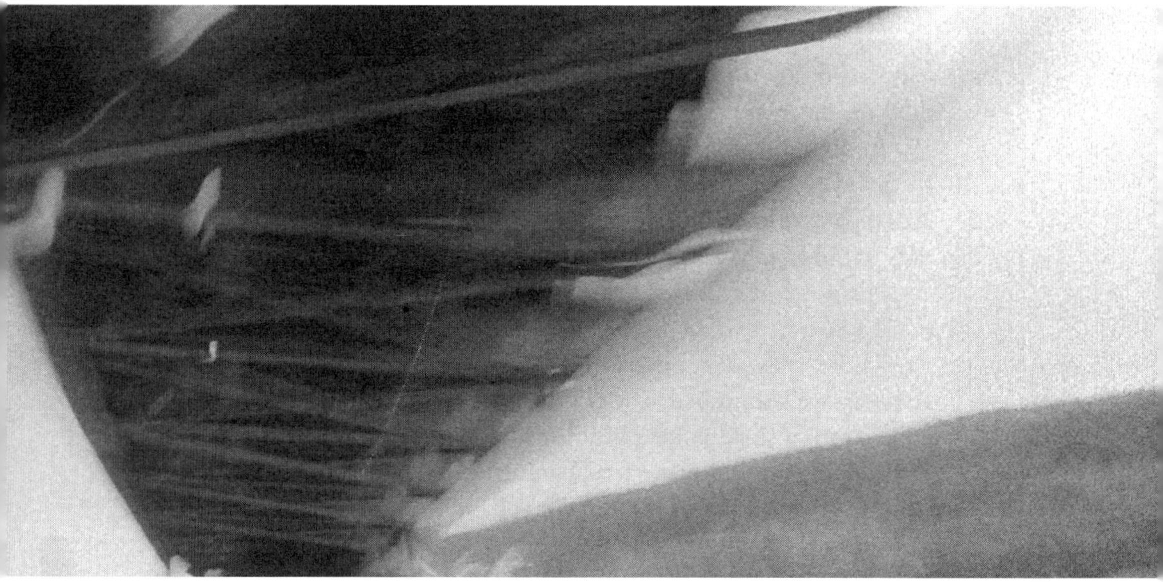

When I Was Mortal

I often pretended to believe in ghosts, in a festive way, and now that I am one I understand why tradition represents them as being in pain and insistent upon returning to the places they knew when they were mortal. The truth is that they do go back. They – or we – are rarely seen, the houses we live in are changed and the new tenants have no knowledge of our past existence, not even a conception of it: like children, these men and women believe the world began with their birth and never wonder if the ground they walk on once felt the touch of lighter footsteps or of an embittered pacing, if between the walls that house them other people heard whispers or laughter, or if anyone read a letter out loud or threw his arm around the neck of the person he loved most. It is absurd that, for the living, space remains and time is erased, while the reality is that space is the depository of time, only it is silent and tells nothing. It is absurd that things should be that way for the living, because what comes afterward is the exact opposite, and nothing has prepared us for it. In other words, now time does not go by, it does not elapse, it does not flow; it is perpetuated simultaneously and in every detail, and to say "now" is perhaps a fallacy. That is the second worst thing, the details, because the representation of what we lived through, of things that barely left a trace on us when we were mortal, now reappears with the horrendous additional element that now everything has meaning and impact: the words spoken without much thought, the automatic gestures, the childhood afternoons we used to lump together that now parade past each other, individualized; the effort of a lifetime to achieve routines that level off the days as well as the nights turns out to have been in vain, and every day, every night is remembered with excessive sharpness and singularity and a degree of reality that is incongruent with our state, which is no longer aware of the tactile. Everything is concrete, excessive, and the knife-edge of repetitions is a torment, because the curse consists in remembering *everything*, all the minutes of every hour of each day that was lived, those of tedium and those of work and those of happiness, those of study and heavyheartedness and degradation and sleep, and also those of waiting, which made up the largest part.

But as I said, that is only the second worst thing; there is something even more lacerating, which is that now I not only remember what I saw and heard and learned of when I was mortal, I remember it whole, in other words including what I did not see or know of or hear then, what was not within my reach but affected me or those who were important to me and who may have shaped me. You now discover the magnitude of what you gradually begin to sense as you live, more and more the more adult you become (I cannot say the older you become, because I never had the chance to grow old): that you know only a fragment of what happens to you, and that when you think you can explain to yourself or tell yourself what has happened up to a given day, you are lacking too much information, you lack the intentions of others and the motives behind the impulses, you lack what is concealed: we see the beings who are closest to us appear as if they were actors suddenly emerging against the backdrop of a theater without our knowing what they were doing until the second before, when they were not in front of us. Perhaps they present themselves disguised as Othello or Hamlet when only a moment ago they were having an impossible anachronistic cigarette backstage and looking impatiently at a watch they have now taken off in order to give the appearance of being another person. We also lack the events at which we are not present and the conversations we do not hear, those that take place behind our backs and mention us or criticize us or judge and condemn us. Life is merciful, all lives are merciful, or that is the norm, and for that reason we consider those who do not cover up or conceal or lie to be malevolent, those who tell all they know and all they hear, all they think and all they do. We say that they are cruel. And the state I find myself in now is a state of cruelty.

I see myself, for example, as a child on the verge of falling asleep in my bed on so many nights during a childhood without upheavals, a satisfactory childhood, with the door of my room ajar so I can see the light until I give in to sleep, so I can grow drowsy listening to the conversation of my father and my mother and one guest or another invited for dinner or for dessert, in the latter case almost always Dr. Arranz, a pleasant man who was always smiling and spoke from between his teeth and who, to my contentment, arrived just before I fell asleep, in time to come into my room and see how I was, the privilege of an almost daily checkup and the doctor's hand that soothes and probes beneath the pajamas, a cool and unrepeatable hand that touches in a way no other hand will for the rest of our lives, and if the child is apprehensive that some abnormality or danger will be detected by it and intercepted, it is the hand that comes to the rescue; and hanging from the ears is the stethoscope with its cold wholesome touch on the flinching chest and sometimes, too, the inherited silver spoon with engraved initials upside down on the tongue, the handle that for a moment seemed it was going to be stuck down our throat, a sensation that yields to the relief of remembering, after the first touch, that it was Arranz who was holding it, his hand that was reassuring and firm and in perfect control of all metallic objects, nothing could happen while he auscultated or scrutinized with the light on his forehead. After his quick visit and his two or three jokes – at times my mother was waiting for him, leaning against the doorway while he examined me and made me laugh easily, and she was amused, too – I was even more lulled and began to drift off as I heard them chatting in the front room which was not far away or heard them listening to the radio for awhile or playing cards a little, in a time during which time barely passed – it seems impossible because it was not so long ago, although from then to now there has been time for me to live and die. I hear the laughter of those who were still young although I could not see them that way then but now I can: my father was the one who laughed least, a handsome taciturn man with a bit of permanent melancholy in his eyes, perhaps because he had been on the side of the Republic and had lost the war, and that must be something you never recover from, losing a war against your own countrymen. He was a good-hearted man who never scolded me or my mother and spent a lot of time in the house writing articles and book reviews for the newspapers, which he usually signed with made-up names, or else reading – he loved French literature, novels by Camus and Simenon are what I remember best. Dr. Arranz was more jovial, a bantering man with a roguish way of speaking, full of imagination and clever phrases, the kind of man children idolize because he knows how to do sleights of hand with cards and entertains them with unexpected rhymes and talks to them about soccer – back then it was Kopa, Rial, Di Stéfano, Puskas and Gento – and he comes up with games that stir their imaginations and tantalize them, since he never has time to stay and really play. And my mother, always well-dressed, though there could not have been much money in the house of a man who had lost the war – and there was not – better dressed than my father because she still had her own father, my grandfather, to dress her, slender and laughing and gazing at her husband, sometimes with pain, gazing at me with enthusiasm always – and neither are there many other gazes like that one later on, as you grow older. I see all this now, but I see it whole, I see that the laughter coming from the front room never came from my father while I was sinking into sleep, but that it was he and he alone who listened to the radio, an impossible image until only a short while ago and now it is as sharp as the older ones that were becoming increasingly compressed and blurry while I was mortal, more and more so the more I lived. I see that on some nights Dr. Arranz and my mother went out, and now I understand all the references to "good tickets," which then I always imagined torn in half by an attendant at a stadium or the bullring – those places where I did not go – and which otherwise I never wondered about. Other nights there were no good tickets, or they were not spoken of, or they were rainy nights that made going out for a stroll or to an evening party seem uninviting, and now I know that then my mother and Dr. Arranz would go into the bedroom when it was certain that I had fallen asleep after having been touched on the chest and the stomach by the same hands that went on to touch her, no longer cool and with much greater urgency, the doctor's hand that soothes and probes and persuades and demands; and also after being kissed on the cheek or the forehead by the same lips that then would kiss – and would forever keep silent about it – that way of speaking between the teeth, self-assured. And whether they went out to the theater or the movies or the dance hall or only went into the next room, my father would put on the radio by himself as he waited, in order not to hear anything, but also, over the course of time and routine, over the course of the leveling-off of the nights that always happens, for the nights insist on repeating themselves, as a distraction for half an hour or forty-five minutes (doctors are always in a hurry), because in the end he was distracted by what he heard. The doctor would leave without saying goodbye to him, and my mother would not come back out of the bedroom, she stayed there waiting for my father, she put on a nightgown and changed the sheets, he never found her there in her pretty skirts and stockings. And I now see the conversation that established this state which for me was not one of cruelty but a merciful one that lasted my entire life, and in this conversation Dr. Arranz sports a small clipped moustache that I would someday see on members of Parliament until Franco's death, and not only on them but also on the military men and the notaries, the bankers and the professors, the writers and many doctors, although not on him, he was one of the first to shave his off. My father and my mother are seated in the dining room, and I do not yet have consciousness or memory, I am a child who does not walk or talk and who is in his crib and who would never have a reason to become aware of this: she keeps her gaze lowered throughout and never says a word, his eyes are first incredulous and then horrified, horrified and more fearful than irate. And one of the things Arranz says is this:

"Look, León, I send a lot of reports to the police, and my family always goes to Mass, they've never missed it. It has taken me too long to get around to you, but I'm well aware of what you did during the war, and you certainly did your share of informing the militiamen so they could make their rounds. But even if you hadn't. In your case I don't have to invent much, just a little exaggeration will be enough, saying you sent half the neighborhood to the gutters wouldn't be too far from the truth, you would have sent me there if you could have. More than ten years have gone by, but you'll get the firing squad if I go ahead with this and I have no reason to keep quiet. So it's up to you to say what you want: either you give in to my conditions and spend a bad moment or two, or you don't and then you have no more moments to spend, good, bad, or so-so."

"And what are your conditions?"

I see Dr. Arranz make a movement of his head toward my silent mother – a gesture that makes her a thing – my mother whom he also knew from the war and from before, also from that neighborhood that lost so many neighbors.

"I get to fuck her. One night and the next, too, until I'm tired of it."

Arranz got tired of it as we get tired of everything, if we are given the time. He "got tired" when I was still at an age when that verb, which is so basic, does not figure in your vocabulary and you have no concept of its contents. My mother, however, was at the age when she began to lose her bloom and not to laugh, and my father began to prosper and dress better and sign the articles and reviews with his own name – his own name, which was not León – and to lose a little of the melancholy in his turbid eyes and go out at night with a pair of good tickets while my mother stayed home to play solitaire or listen to the radio or soon after that to watch television, increasingly resigned.

Those who have speculated on the afterlife or the persistence of consciousness beyond death – if that is what we are, consciousness – have not taken into account the danger or rather the horror of remembering everything, even what we did not know, of knowing everything, everything that had to do with us or that we were in the middle of or perhaps only close to. I see with absolute clarity faces I walked past only once in the street, a beggar I gave some change to without looking him in the face, a woman I saw riding the subway and never thought of again, the features of a messenger who brought me an unimportant telegram, the figure of a little girl I saw on a beach when I was a little boy. The long minutes I spent waiting in airports or standing in line in a museum or watching the water on that distant beach or packing my bags and then unpacking them later are all repeated, the most tedious minutes, those that never tell us anything, those we call dead time. I see myself in cities where I spent only a short time long ago, with a few free hours to stroll through them and then erase them from my memory; I see myself in Hamburg and in Manchester, in Basel and in Austin, in places I would never have gone if my work hadn't taken me there. I also see myself in Venice, so long ago, on my honeymoon with my wife Luisa, whom I have spent these last years of calm and contentment with, I see myself during those years, in my most recent life, though it is already remote. I come back from a trip and she is waiting for me at the airport, there was not one time in our marriage when she was not there to pick me up, even if I had been away only a couple of days, despite the abominable traffic and the unnecessary activities, which are always the most fatiguing. I would usually be so tired that I only had the energy to change channels in front of the television, the same as all televisions in all of our countries, while she prepared a little dinner and then joined me in eating it with a bored but patient expression, knowing I needed only the lethargy and the coming night's rest to recover and be the man I always was the next day, an active joking fellow who talked between his teeth a little in a studied way, accentuating the irony that all women like, they have laughter in their blood and cannot keep from laughing even if they hate the person making the joke, if the joke is funny. And the following afternoon, now fully recovered, I would go to see María, my mistress, who would laugh even harder because for her my witty remarks were not worn out.

I was always careful not to give myself away, not to wound, and to be merciful, I saw María only at her house so that no one could ever run into me anywhere with her and ask questions or be cruel and talk about it later or simply expect to be introduced. Her house was nearby and I spent a lot of afternoons there on my way home, not every afternoon; it meant a delay of only half an hour or forty-five minutes, sometimes a little more, sometimes I lingered there looking out of her window, our mistress' window has an interest that our own will never have. I never made a mistake, because mistakes in these matters are a form of inconsideration or, even worse, acts of malevolence. Once I crossed paths with María while I was with Luisa, at a crowded movie theater on the opening night of a new film, and my mistress took advantage of the commotion to approach us and take my hand for an instant; walking past me without looking at me, she brushed me with the thigh I knew so well and took my hand and stroked it. Luisa could never have seen it or have noticed or have had the least suspicion of this tenuous, ephemeral, and clandestine contact, but even so I decided not to see María for several weeks, at the end of which, because I did not answer her calls to my office, she called me one afternoon at my house; fortunately, my wife was not there.

"What's going on?" she said.

"You must never call me here, you know that."

"I wouldn't call you there if you would pick up for me in your office," she said. "I've been waiting for two weeks."

And I answered, making an effort to recover the fury I had sustained for those two weeks, "I'll never pick up for you again if you touch me in front of Luisa one more time. Don't even let the idea cross your mind."

She was silent.

Almost everything in life is forgotten, and everything is remembered in death or in that state of cruelty which being a ghost consists of. But in life I forgot and went back to seeing her one day and then the next one, too, in the same way that everything is indefinitely put off a short while and we always believe that there is still a tomorrow in which it will be possible to bring an end to what goes by and elapses and flows, today and yesterday, what imperceptibly becomes another routine which in its own way also levels off our days and our nights until finally they are inconceivable without any of the elements that have been installed in them, and the nights and days must be identical at least in their essential components, so that there will be neither renunciation nor sacrifice, neither those who demand them nor those who endure them. Everything is remembered now, and therefore I remember my death perfectly, too, in other words, what I knew about my death when it took place, which was not very much or nothing at all if I compare it with the totality of my knowledge now and the knife-edge of repetitions.

I came back from one of my exhausting trips and Luisa did not fail me, she came to pick me up. We did not talk much in the car or while I was mechanically unpacking my bag and casting a very cursory glance at the accumulated mail and listening to the messages kept on the answering machine for my return. One of them alarmed me because I instantly recognized María's voice, which spoke my name once and was then cut off, which lessened my alarm immediately, a woman's voice saying my name and then breaking off meant nothing, there was no reason for it to have disturbed Luisa if she had heard it. I stretched out on the bed in front of the television and watched some programs, Luisa brought me a store-bought meal of cold meat, she must not have had the time or felt like making me even an omelette. It was still early, but she turned the bedroom light off to get me to go to sleep, and there I was, drowsy and lulled by the vague memory of her caresses, the hand that soothes even when it touches the chest distractedly and perhaps with impatience, and then she left the bedroom and I ended up falling asleep with the television set on; there was a moment when I stopped changing channels.

I do not know how much time went by, except I'm lying, since now I do know exactly how much, seventy-three minutes of deep sleep and dreams that were still set in the foreign country I had returned from safe and sound once more. Then I woke up and saw the bluish light from the television illuminating the foot of the bed rather than any of the images on the screen, because I did not have time for that. I see and saw hurtling down on my forehead something black, an object that was heavy and undoubtedly as cold as the stethoscope, but it was not wholesome, it was violent. It fell once and rose again, and in those tenths of a second before it smashed back down, now spattered with blood, I thought that Luisa was killing me because of the phone call that only said my name and then broke off and perhaps had said many more things that she had erased after listening to all of them, leaving me to hear on my return only the beginning, only the announcement of what was killing me. The black thing fell again and this time it killed, and my last living consciousness kept me from putting up any resistance or trying to stop her, because she was unstoppable, and perhaps also because it did not seem like a bad way to die, this death at the hands of the person with whom I had lived in calm and contentment and without hurting each other until finally we did. The word is difficult and lends itself to equivocations, but perhaps I reached the point of feeling that this was a just death.

I see all of this now and I see it whole, with an afterward and a before, although the afterward has nothing to do with me in the strictest sense and for that reason it does not turn out to be as painful. But the before is painful, or rather the negation of what I glimpsed and was about to think between the lowering and the raising and again the lowering of the black thing that finished me off. I now see Luisa talking to a man I do not know, who sports a moustache like the one Dr. Arranz sported in his day, although it is not clipped, but soft and thick and showing a few white hairs. He is a middle-aged man, the same age as I was and perhaps as Luisa was, too, although I always saw her as a young woman, in the same way that I could never see my parents and Arranz as young. They are together in the living room of a house I do not recognize either, which is his house, a motley place full of books and paintings and decorations, a studied place. The man is named Manolo Reyna and he has enough money to keep him from ever having to get his hands dirty. They are speaking in whispers, sitting on a sofa, it is late in the afternoon and I am at that very moment visiting María, two weeks before, two weeks from my death on my return from a trip, and that trip has not yet begun, preparations for it are still underway. The whispers are now very clear, they have a degree of reality that is incongruent not with my state, which is not aware of the tactile, but with life itself, nothing in life is ever this concrete, nothing breathes this much. But there is a moment when Luisa raises her voice, as you raise it to defend yourself or to defend someone else, and what she says is this:

"But he has always been very good to me, he has given me nothing to complain about, so it's very difficult."

And Manolo Reyna answers, dragging out his words:

"It wouldn't be any easier or cost you any less if he had made your life impossible. When the time comes to kill someone, whatever he may have done doesn't count, it always seems like too excessive an act for any kind of behavior."

I see Luisa lift her thumb to her mouth and nibble it a little, a gesture I have seen her make so many times when she is hesitating, or before she decides on something, a trivial gesture, and it is shattering to see that it still appears in the middle of a conversation at which we were not present, a conversation that takes place behind our back and mentions us or criticizes us or even defends us, or judges us and condemns us to death.

"You kill him then. You wouldn't want me to commit such an excessive act."

I now see, too, that the person who is grasping the black thing next to my flickering television is not Luisa, nor is it Manolo Reyna with his folkloric name, but someone hired and paid to make it come smashing down twice on my forehead, what is called a hatchet man, during the war many members of the militia were used for that. My hatchet man strikes twice and strikes with dispassion, and this death no longer seems just to me, nor fitting, nor, of course, merciful, as life usually is and as mine was. The black thing is a hammer with a wooden handle and an iron head, an ordinary hammer. It's the hammer I keep in the house, I recognize it.

There where time still elapses and flows, a great deal of time has passed already, so much that none of those I knew or dealt with or endured or desired remains. Every one of them, I suppose, will return unseen to this space in which forgotten time accumulates and will see there nothing but strangers, new men and women who believe, like children, that the world began with their birth and for whom it is senseless to wonder about our existence, which is over and has been swept away. Now Luisa will remember and know what she did not know when she was alive, nor when I was dead. I cannot speak of nights or days now, everything is leveled off without the need for any effort or for the routines in which I can say that I knew calm and contentment more than anything else, when I was mortal, so long ago, there where there is still time.

Translated from Spanish by Esther Allen

Jáchym *TOPOL*

Time can be kept in objects. Canissa taught me how. In those days I kept my time tucked away in shiny shards of glass in the pockets of my shorts. I would sit in class or at home and unwrap a piece of glass from my handkerchief and watch it as time started to unwind, gently at first, like a feather floating to the ground (later Canissa taught me that in fact the reason why feathers are so good for storing pieces of time is precisely because of their gentleness), and then the time in the glass would start to accelerate, and I was there in it with Little White Canissa, with the grass and the trees in our hole in the hillside, with her touches, I was there in real life.

She saw the green eyes of the woman I was going to meet in the future, which gifted women can see. She'll probably be a wrestler, said Canissa one day in bed, testing her bruises. I won't toss and turn anymore, I said. Oh yes you will, she said back.

With Little White Canissa I was no one, just a shape born of steam, of wind, of dampness. She caressed nerves I didn't even know I had, my face took on a new appearance, I began to feel my body. I began to dance. Just stretching your hand muscles is dancing for a cripple. She pulled me in, formed me, and that in turn was what made her foundation.

Our fondling, culminating first in an orgasm for me and then, much later, for her, was more than just a giving and receiving of pleasure, it was the ritual of a tribe under siege. Like all of my loves, Little White Canissa had black hair; I called her white because of her skin. In my thoughts I still call her that, even now, after everything I'm trying to capture here disappeared, and I met Sister, and Little White Canissa turned into a ghost, a good she-demon with inscrutable intentions.

We slept together and played together, lived together in fact, but the main thing was to fight the flood of filth and nothingness. The magic remained somewhere beneath the surface, glowing inside her like lumps of coal, and I think I had it in me too, only cooler, like amber, and sometimes when we spent a long time by ourselves it would appear, and the next time I saw the red darkness was the day we went to see the Germans.

Here I am handing out cookies to these guys like some senior citizen when what we really oughta be doing is pounding the hell out of em, said Sinkule.

The cops were pulling down some scrawny insubordinate guy in a suit from the wall over the entrance to the Embassy. He wanted to take a shortcut and resisted; they beat him with their clubs. He got up from the ground and obediently joined the procession of other Germans patiently pacing back and forth in front of the Embassy waiting their turn. There were thousands of them, stretching in rows through the crooked streets and down to the square, where for days now traffic had been brought to a stop.

Hey, here they come again, Sinkule slugged me in the shoulder. A row of white helmets with long clubs began setting up barricades in the middle of the crowd. The Germans who were separated from the Embassy started to get nervous; the crowd tensed up in the fear that this was the end, this was the selection. Letting out a howl the crowd leaned into the cordon as mothers passed children over the cops' helmets to the people on the other side, probably their relatives, it occurred to me.

Once the child's inside they probably let the mother in too, sure, but it's not like the kids have ID, so how are the mothers going to prove who's theirs? And what if one of them grabs someone else's kid? How will they settle it then? Like that Jewish dude Solomon?

Let's roll, come on.

No need, said Sinkule, it'll calm down soon. The cops don't care about the Germans. I've got the whole thing cased. They'll keep hassling folks for awhile and then pull out. All they want to do is make sure us locals know they're here.

Well I don't want to get it and I'd rather not stick around to watch.

Take it easy, they'll never get as far as us.

Sinkule had been at the Embassy every day, he was one of those people who were fascinated by the exodus.

Anyway, you look German, they'll leave you alone, he said, glancing at me. You speak German?

Nah, just stuff like hende hok, los shvine, achtung minen, arbyte makt fry, all that crap from the movies. And myne leebe komen fiken, never did use that one though.

Sinkule was right, the cops were pulling out, and an eerie silence again settled over the crowd surrounding the Embassy.

What about me, you think I look German?

You? I nearly busted out laughing. Yeah, and Goebbels was German too.

But I can speak it, my mom was German.

Here they are, back again.

As a rule, the cops wouldn't risk moving into the crowd via the narrow passage from the Rychta beer hall above the square. And if they did, then only in large numbers. The Germans were silent. The ones in front walked slowly, struggling up the slope, while the rest tried to step in place at least. Ordinarily a crowd murmurs, the individual utterances intertwining with one another, it's a little like water, you have to lap up the words. But these people were silent, as if they had decided they weren't going to speak until they reached the other side of the gate. Just then someone in the crowd broke into loud laughter. Then a child broke into tears. Then another one. And suddenly the square was full of crying children, it had never occurred to me before that in a way they were like dogs: once one starts, all the others join in. But these kids weren't crying on account of some stupid Czech cops. Some of them had been on the road for days now, in overcrowded trains, in Trabants and Wartburgs loaded high with junk, hungry, hadn't had a good night's sleep, and they could sense their parents' nervousness.

Suddenly an officer lost his temper and knocked a thermos from the hand of an elderly Czech woman who had been pouring tea for the Germans. Where's your permit? he screamed. Another ripple ran through the crowd, and in a blink the old woman found herself alone.

That's old Vohryzková from our building, said Sinkule. That cunt, at least now she'll stop going around like she's Mother Theresa.

Give it to her good, you brute! he hollered at the cop, and we ran for it.

Thank God they always send the hicks into Prague, we'd never have made it through the passageways otherwise.

Just to be sure, I crossed myself. We came out through the passageway under the church with the Bambino di Praga, gasping for breath.

Hey Sinkule, you notice they've started closing up the passages?

Yeah, that's what did me in. I been crawling through the things all my city rat life and those fuckers go and close em up on me. You're the only one I'm telling this, I'm goin too. I'm telling you so you can watch out for me so I don't end up somewhere in some hole.

You mean you wanna ditch it with the Germans?

Yeah, Šulc made it already, he's inside right now. He just went yesterday and he's already inside.

What, are you nuts? I mean, this is the end!

Nobody knows that. The Germans are going over to the Germans, but there's no way our guys are gonna let us make the grab here at home. I got it all scoped out, me and Majsner are gonna go together, I mean, half of us here are German anyway. No one's checking anything, and if they do I'll just say they took my papers at the border, the Embassy's such a mess they're just stickin em in the buses and shippin em out. I'll send some chocolate and come back for you driving a white tank.

So the Bambino di Praga was where it began. We walked back to the square and up to the Embassy. They waited a long time. I saw them being let in.

Glaser made it through too, he sat a year after they caught him under the wires in Šumava, he lay buried in the sand all day suffocating with the mosquitoes eating him alive, but he chose the wrong time to crawl out and they left him hogtied for hours...in a cell full of shit...but now he was passing through the gate and just for good measure he spit on one of the Commie cops, the Germans picked up on it and as soon as they set foot inside the gate they turned around and spit on him too, soon he started to look like he was covered with sperm, his club hung impotently from his belt, he was afraid... It was weird, my first step into freedom and instead of breathing it in I spit on someone, Glaser told me afterward.

Others went too, mostly people who actually did have German blood in their family...but even that idiot Novák got in – first he got in and then he left and went over to U Schnellů for a beer just because he liked the idea of being able to come and go as he pleased.

In the streets the crowd dragged slowly and sluggishly, the young long-haired Germans in packs, boys leading girls, holding hands sometimes like me and Canissa, only they were going somewhere else...old women with purses, families with little children carrying teddy bears and dolls in their arms...but once there was room in the streets with only bunches of people walking, alarming reports caught up to them from all over the city, or maybe it was just strange vibrations from the train stations, from Dresden, Karl-Marx Stadt, Gera, Zwickau, villages and small towns along the border, from the households where they were hurriedly packing last things, jewelry, packing food and clothes and for the hundredth time for the last time nervously looking over their passports and setting out, the Monster could reawaken at any moment, refreshed and ready to dish out the punishment...and the bunches picked up their pace, the last hundred, twenty, ten meters some of them even broke into a run...on the streets of Malá Strana they left behind bags and suitcases too heavy to carry, blankets they had huddled in overnight when the Embassy got too crowded, inflatable pillows, propane-butane tanks, a teddy bear with its head twisted backward, plastic dolls lost in the confusion, no doubt replaced by that bitch Barbie...I saw a frying pan and a school bag, the square below the Embassy was filled with German cars, a Trabant was lying on its side with a down quilt on its roof...

Stride after stride
Their pots and pans knock at their sides
Their children on carts piled high with quilts ride
Crosses burning up in the sky
Days with salty anguish come undone
No one at all can tell them why
Or where to now or what will come.

Well, it's not as dramatic as all that.

That's Hanuš Bonn, said Little White Canissa. Only these porky pigs from the gee-dee-ar aren't striding into any blazing ovens.

Hey, they're going into the unknown, they're fugitives, I mean, look at those two old ladies holding each other up.

Yeah, exactly.

So what do you mean? Are you telling me she's some kind of Ilsa Koch? And that granddad there is Mengele, is that it?

I know it's stupid, said Canissa, but Germans piss me off, I can't help it. Their language pisses me off. I went to the train station this morning to help, but still they piss me off. They say my grandpa weighed 40 kilos when he got back. Not for long. Bonn was a family friend, we've got a copy of *Voice in the Distance* with a dedication from him. Anyway, it's the Communists' fault for fucking us up with all those movies, I never actually even talked with one of them.

Till today.

That's right. Some cab drivers are driving them in here for free, but others are ripping them off like crazy.

Some like you help them, some break into their cars.

That's the thing about the human tribe, like we said when we were little... Canissa stretched her red lips wide and wiggled her tongue... The thing is that whenever things are happening, that's when the people of a tribe recognize each other. People divide in moments of danger. Everything's fine until the moment when something's at stake.

And what's at stake here, Canissa?

I dunno, God maybe, or maybe everything. There's all kinds of paths and everyone has to choose for himself.

That's our pact.

The pact's valid, but we're not going to be scared.

Of what, machine guns on the roof? I'll probably never stop being scared of them.

She shoved open the door of a building that had a lion in its coat-of-arms.

Here there was the sweet smell of wood, somewhere else there was a cesspool, we picked cellars because we longed for that hole in the ground where she had taught me and where the world became real for the very first time, where our bodies grew up together and where each of us knew every inch of our own body and the other's as they got bigger and rougher... cellars also conserved time, inviolate and compacted, in the corners and under vaults, in the nooks and crannies, and it was also in the spiderwebs, which served as the delicate dress for this wedding. Down there it was often wet with water, time had a heavy scent, it slaked our thirst. I would hold Canissa on top of me or she'd sit in an alcove and spread her legs, and then, in the clench of male and female, in the movement, the swaying, all at once the rhythm would come and that brought the red darkness and that was where the pictures were. We made the time around us move, it whirled and spoke to me. Sometimes Canissa would whisper into my ear, today she spoke of fear, and every time she ran her nails down my flanks, slicing my skin, it was like lightning bolts flashing down through the darkness under my eyelids, the sounds in the red darkness forming letters, the speech of fear, the fear of the masses, it's sour, I could hear Canissa's brain echoing. We knew that time flowed up above too, but we no longer had the power to reach that high...up to the rooftops where there might be machine guns...and then again there might not be...but it wasn't so much them actually, there was also a nest up there where mutated pigeons were born with the plague and the little ones fell out of it, freaks full of chemicals, the first time they tried to fly they fell to the cobblestones without any protection, nobody heard them, nobody except for maybe Old Bog, and they were born with nothing but terror and no hope.

We aged in those twilights, and the power of my Canissa turned against her because she was no longer living just for herself, not anymore, she wanted to move on and take me with her. But I was afraid to live in this world the way she pictured it, to give it to her, to be in someone else...my power faded as I acted, I could only feel the world in assorted costumes and roles because the thought of direct contact filled me with fear.

We screwed in cellars whenever we could, we became absolute virtuosos at finding places where it was warm and dark and old time murmured like a living thing. When a lion mates with a lioness he grips the nape of her neck so tightly with his teeth that her neck would break if she moved, that was how we held on to each other with every pore. And the red darkness was still there even when I opened my eyelids. Canissa just watched with a smile on her face, she knew already, for a long time probably, that the red darkness came from inside us but also existed out there in the world, like the animals and the deserts and the shit of the tenants who lived in the maze of apartments above. We were shielded by a cloud that was firmly fastened to the dark around the edges, sometimes an electric light would flash by in the dark when they came down for coal…

Suddenly I heard the clink of shovel on pail, clear as a string, and then she sent me on my way to the old woman. As I sank into Canissa with my eyes, I saw myself, first as a small marble, then as a microscopic Gulliver, I passed through every wrinkle in the skin of the old woman's face, every fold I felt. In my own eyes, fixed on the smiling eyes of Canissa, I saw my terror as I traveled along the skin of the old woman's belly, and she sent me even further, in time too, my body touched the damp germ cells and was no longer my body, I had become part of the embryo, I was inside, time had abruptly turned around and I could feel time stop as the pain came, and the pain was what made reality, and then Canissa sent me back out into the old lady's innards, they opened up to me and I was on my way back out again, and then I was inside Canissa and I could feel the pressure in my cock. As I spurted into her I wished I could go all the way down to the bottom and out, but she was holding me firmly in place…and then I could feel life-time, that old time in the subterranean spaces we frequented, starting to steal us away, we slipped out of the alcove and flew through the air, Canissa's body grew heavy in my arms, I could see her face sagging, her hair going gray. Her skin was rough, I touched her belly, scarred from childbirth… I won't show you yourself! was the sentence she gave me.

We walked out of the building and back onto the set. A rumbling sound came from the square, as if all those Trabants that had become such a fixture there were suddenly starting up at once. Maybe it's the vans, I thought. Maybe they're sending in a few tanks after all. Canissa adjusted her skirt.

Listen, I'm just *not* going to wear them, I mean they're always damp.

You should've left them there.

What, are you crazy? Some pervert warlock finds them and we're goners.

There had been a time when she didn't wear panties on our walks, but then I realized that I enjoyed it more when I had to fuck through them, running my cock up her thigh and then trapping it under the elastic, the touch of the fabric, the resistance of the elastic excited me. The fact is that Canissa really *was* little, so the extra distance it created between me and her vagina was negligible. And maybe in those days, as I was losing her, my penis needed to feel something besides her, it didn't matter what. And maybe her grip was getting weaker as she lost her power. And then again, maybe I just wasn't as young as I used to be, and my cock demanded rougher treatment.

It was buses. Dozens of buses sitting in rows, one after the next, filled with Germans. But they weren't the same, this wasn't the nervous herd pacing back and forth in front of the Embassy. I could make out individual faces, each with its own expression, they weren't just faces in the crowd anymore. They were elsewhere now, they were in their own time and it wasn't sour, they ceased to interest me.

Hey, said Canissa, I saw Šulc! So he made it!

You knew?

Yeah, he came over all freaked out and said he wanted to learn how to say "They took my papers" in Deutsch. Had a faint ready too, just in case.

And how do you say it?

Don't ask me. I didn't realize he was serious. I must've made him repeat "Ich bin der auslender" a hundred times.

As the buses drove off one by one, the bystanders filled the square. From the neighboring streets they came, out of shops and pubs, they came to watch. From homes too, people emerged to join the silent demonstration under the cover of the archways, where some had been standing for hours, and watch the Germans leave. The ones in the last buses no longer had that look of fugitive foreigners, of strangers trapped in a strange city, they were smiling, and some of them looked like they enjoyed waving to the crowd. A hand poked out of one of the bus windows holding a can of Coca-Cola. Three boys suddenly jumped in to vie for the prize; clawing the can from the hand, the biggest of the three stuffed it under his jacket and ran. The other two went on wandering along the buses until someone tossed them a pack of gum, they stood absorbed with splitting it up until finally the driver of one of the buses bound for Paradise tore them out of their trance with a honk of his horn like a fart during mass. Not a word from the Czechs while the Germans in the last bus smiled happy and weary, some of them flashed the V sign, they looked like passengers on a charter excursion now. And the people on the streets, the ones who had clogged up the buses' route, the ones who walked a few steps behind the last departing bus to stealthily occupy the space where all it took was a turn of the key in the ignition to clear the iron hurdle, suddenly all it took to reach the border was a few steps along the cobblestones...

Descending the streets from the Castle, the heavy-clad cops were closing in again.

Only this time it wasn't with the routine stride of extras from some movie about the Crusades, these guys were running. I couldn't catch sight of their faces behind the plexiglass, but from the way they were moving it was obvious they were eager. The wild boars had caught a whiff of the watering hole, a jungle scene came to me so I danced it with my feet and grabbed hold of Little White Canissa, she was already crouching, she'd picked up on their scent. The first row of cops had their clubs out and ready. No foreigners here now, no cameras to spoil the dictatorship's rep.

And we're gone, I said more forcefully than usual.

Slowly at first, then faster and faster, the crowd began to disperse, no one waited for the head-on collision, what had once been a menacing monolithic mass was reduced in an instant to mere clusters, and then only individuals, and all of a sudden everything was as before, here and there a senior citizen, a harmless student, a worker in coveralls, a mother with a baby carriage, everyone in their usual roles, the familiar creak of pub doors. Once again the trams stopped on the square. Jícha materialized in front of me and Canissa.

Ciao, Bára, ciao, Potok! Wow, you saw it! Pinch me if I'm dreaming!

A perfect time loop, said Canissa. She's an expert in these matters, my love is.

What a demonstration! That was great! Those cops were scared stiff, Jícha said gleefully.

What are you up to today? I said out of curiosity.

Nothing, he said truthfully.

Come see our performance, we can sneak you in somehow, I said condescendingly.

What? You mean you're putting on a show?

Uh-huh.

You know that Jirmut's back in the clink and Pečorka too? And they locked up the Slovaks. There were strikes in theaters all over Poland when they put Solidarity behind bars! And here?

Huh, that didn't occur to me, said Bára.

Somebody's gotta start here too, you know, said Jícha.

That got my attention... *Start*... Half-assed activists like this guy though...

But... I said.

You could be the ones, said Jícha.

But... I said.

We're just a small company of perverts, Canissa said, coming to the rescue.

No thanks, I've got something on for tonight, see ya round, said Jícha.

See ya, we said.

Let's go for a coffee, Bára, I'm battered and beat.

Not me. You're getting old.

I dunno. I'm going.

Alright then. Later.

Later.

I set out after her, watching the street, and when we passed the building with the sign, it seemed suited, so I spoke up again. That's where we were. And you, Canissa, on your way, you moved, arched, slipped round the corner, that's how I'll put it, she slipped round the corner and I guess kept on going, I guess, though actually she might have flown off into time, maybe she used that trick with the power she taught me way back at a boring party we went to, where you stick your fingers into the socket and reverse the current with your power and go with it, and you see the lines in your brain, the colorful lines of the current's power as they pass through the entire building, and you go through all the outlets, all the walls, and then you stop the current with your fingers so the lines circle back all the way around and wind into each other and you go, it's a closed field and you can run in it for as long as your breath holds out. For as long as you want it to, if you want it to. It's a colorful game. I'm going to say it: you grabbed hold of me in the cellar and held on...and maybe you were playing that way now, with the outlet maybe, with air, with stone, with some other male, with someone you just met, because we put on the show without you that evening and the next time I saw you wasn't till years later, if I refer to time in conventional terms.

I missed her during the show because that was my piece, a piece I wrote for her or someone else from the community. I played the part of a human rose and I had an hour to bud, blossom, flourish, wither, and wilt. There was a section of short scenes and clever skits, usually it had them rolling in the aisles, off to the side I went on with my subtle role...we mixed in a little porno here and there as part of the battle against the regime, we had the gardener getting the elves all hot to trot... every now and then a child walking across the stage so it'd be obvious the emperor was naked...Little White Canissa was a swarm of flies, voracious aphids, she poked me full of holes. And since Canissa didn't show up that evening, Cepková, the blonde, had to step in, and while she was sawing off my thorns I saw the face of Canissa under her makeup, it sent me a message, and I heard her brain, I was in the rose's red darkness and I knew Canissa wanted to free me of fear, but I didn't want to be freed because then I wouldn't be able to act, without fear I could do anything but create, I chose fear, so Canissa shut me out of the community, cut me off from herself, but she promised to send me Sister to fill my future...and there were two green spots glowing in Cepková's face like magnets, like her face had just been radiated...then the fire went out and the female face beneath the makeup settled back into its clown face for the evening, precisely as the script called for, and Canissa was gone...her message made my tears flow down the rose, the people in the first row, who could see, said to themselves, Potok the dancer, stoned again, but I didn't give a damn, I mean even Nero, that old sadist, needed a cast of thousands for his poem about the fire...and then she danced around me a little, playing the scissors and the greedy hand and the storm with falling tree trunks, then some water and a sunbeam...and the audience went wild...and then she was gone...so after consulting with the stage manager, I stuck a tube in my mouth and wound it around me, it led to a carafe of red wine, that night I drank gallons of it and thought of my girlfriend, if she hadn't showed it must have been serious, and then it was dark. And the next morning I woke up looking at Cepková, the blonde in my bed, pretty damn disgusting, I told myself, I woke her up and told her to hit the road. Only then it struck me, what if Canissa had fulfilled her promise and sent me Sister – so soon? But the touch of those blonde tresses turned my stomach.

Translated from Czech by Alex Zucker

Joaquim *Manuel*

MAGALHÃES

Sloten

Sometimes we wake up happy. The house
is calm, the bedroom looks out
onto an anchorage with fallen stones
and cropped trees and terrace walls.
The coarse wool of the curtains props
the opaque sky above the urban buildings.
The universe, submissive, seems willing
to protect; in its morning it shelters
the facades with their three-windowed,
two-windowed, one-windowed floors; they end
in the mist, in blurred triangles.
The heat radiates from the pipes, the rain
caresses the still boats, a man with a stick
bends over to gather up debris.
Flocks of birds, gentle winds, everything at rest.
I open the room's armor plating and hear
the bricks, the paint, the stairs, the handrail
bleeding.

Boats with furled sails on the street corner.
And his body placidly shimmering
in the ordered abandon of the suburbs;
the regular, millimetric, compressed
apartments of the industrial devastation.

A nearly full glass of beer, a peeled lime,
a cheese with an already missing wedge;
in the midst of napkins, utensils and fruit
a very thinly sliced smoked herring
which a little mustard and butter
will cover with a falsely festive flavor.
Beyond the burlaped window over
the table with a flowered tablecloth
the pincer wakes up among soft and low houses
to pursue the slit terrain.

Still an urban landscape, but now the masts
cross planted fields, and final leaves
hang from branches that divide the skies:

a leaden vegetable stroke waving
over the fixed line of a watery stroke that
separates the meadows, the charcoal of the clouds.
The sunless light disperses in hues
of injured green life.
In the distance; where you were.

The horizon ends in a sylvan color.
The final gray rises up from the depth
that brings the black tumult with hesitant stars
and mineral reverberations.

Saber and sheath,
the gold brush
and the shoehorn,
the silver bowl,
the serving tray,
the worn mirror,
the round case
with mother-of-pearl,
the nail-care kit,
the pewter candlestick
among soup tureens,
the covered dish,
the fish cleaver,
the tongs for meat,
the silver-plated
draining spoon
and gravy spoon,
the squat amphora
of dark enamel
with an inlay,
the jug with no lid,
the black-lacquer box.
And in the hourglass
the time that fell
over an ossuary
with those tiny jars

for sundry excreta,
above which wafts
the heavy smoke
of other essences:
of your fingers that hold me on the precipice,
of your shoulders that carry me through the winter,
of your hair whose strands draw a bay where the
encounter
with you with me the nonencounter with emptiness
sails in the air with uncut stones.

In the close din of the crowd
of windows, the water flows
through slashes which in this moment glow.
Your incredulous face is lost
in the sleeping depth of a photograph.

The steep pulsing of afternoon
lights the equilibrium of love
that no longer wants to speak; it takes refuge
in the painted miniature of the fleeting enchantment.
You pull from your pocket the incense box
with a bone set into the wood
at the entrance to a forest of concrete.
There, why not? we will kiss.

The sky would occasionally rise,
then lower. And in its shadow,
to the thrill of the cold, the bicycles
rode over the uneven stones.
With the pleasure of riding no matter where
and without any hurry to get there.

And after the bridge and the sluice
we'll arrive at the room where the day
will end in water.
With the sepulchral night's
now almost moth-eaten light.

Ensconced lamp, table with rug,
ice of peonies from the yard,
gutted and decapitated animals,
the wick of the knife in the candlestick.
A residue of regurgitated sarcasms
after the last battle.

And when you asked me my age
I told you I was eighty-eight
nightmares old in the place of my voice
and you didn't laugh with your twenty-two
years but said that in that case you were
forty-four, the same as I.
And in that triple progression of two
the traffic of a life went by;
and the greater passage of what in us
another could never have.

Ecce homo; that's what must occur to me
as I undo all of your shirt's buttons.

The café employee said it was ready
to be served, but what?
The nape of your neck? That lonely
hand on top of the worn table
whose knots were blurred from furtive uses
and pretty, deleterious discourses?

Here in this vaulted, nocturnal interior
I cannot say I still possess
the impetus of pain that moved me, in another place,
lit by a bright shining sun near the sea
(how I hate brightness, the sun, and its sea),
to spill out under the cover of alcohol.
But why not tell you – twilight has fallen –
that a certain fire almost at its end
acquires from a consumed inertia
the supreme power of cremation.

Suddenly a dimmer spotlight
shone against the target whose center was lost.
Throw the dart, it's your turn. What are you waiting for?
Do you want me to call all the moves?
And you with skilled hand, strong craftsman's wrist,
and barbed hair over vinyl eyebrows.

Wearing coarse wool trousers and a loud striped shirt,
his raincoat abandoned on a bar stool,
the lute player salutes a time that has passed
and rallies the crowd in the room where drinks,
light meals and the day's last encounters
prepare for tomorrow, for an almost forever
of entrances and exits accompanied by laughs
and looks in which tenderness veers away.

Now it's late. On the sluice
where the slush and the rust
of all the discarded things flow,
the inhabited fog rises past the night.
When you smiled among the oars,
the viscous convulsion of debris
grew into red shrubs with berries
crackling in the shadows;
and an array of invisible birds
flew to no one, in the heights,
with the fluttering of unexpected flames.

The sea inside the tree, the clouds
inside the land without end,
the light. The light inside another light
that captured hands and opened them
to other hands inside a gaze.

The wind singing in the furnace.
A heavy glass goblet with home-
fermented liqueur. A plate
with filberts, walnuts, and arbutus leaves.
On the border the closed shutters

acquire a halo from the streetlamps
which diffuses in the television's fluorescence,
in the pallid red of the radio's tiny lights.

The day's final clarity mingles
with the first of the night.
It won't be the jeweller where the rain beats down
that forces my heart, nor will this hedgerow
flanked by cement suspend the flight
of what I am to what you're not, but the caress
trembling on the belt, the heat of your uncovered
neck, the wicker of the chair from which you stand
as I'm about to sit down.

Between strips of uneven grass,
a pocked embankment shelters
machines of desolation.
Ducks in formation cross
the polished glass of the window.
The day hits the newspaper lying
on the brown blanket that wraps
my knees in the indoor silence.
On another day, the blinds already shut,
a canvas globe illuminates the book,
the table, the flowers hanging by a string
from a beam, and the cabinet
backed with tin and meditation.

Life has piled up on pulleys surrounding everything,
a smoke in the night that hits the map
rolled up on the naked wall, so long have we forgotten
to open it up, to follow its signs to the limits
of our world. Which I lost for you.
And we are already fading.

Newspapers piled in a shallow basket.
On the floor a single wooden sandal
and an absurdly flashy tie
for someone of your repressions.

On a footrest a dog for the blind snoozes
as the vacuum hums in concert with the sound
of the washing machine and the dishes
rattling on top of the refrigerator.
Is it a Dutch or Portuguese interior?
With the picture hanging by a thick cord,
the torn velvet of the sofa, and the shelf
of useless and unforgiving books, perhaps it is
a wasteland of affections, an anyman's land.

Today's sky arches high and is crossed by crows
with a hard mystery in their pilgrim wings
planing over the open grave of the world.
A black tile spire reflects midday;
windmills turn their blades in the distance.
Banal events next to those that will follow.

His heel, his kneecap, his pelvis
were wider than I had imagined
when I saw his lean figure on the stairs;
the land without height called Holland
well suited that body I held in my arms,
that ruthless bell buoy.
There was no one left in the patriarchal sitting room
but us, talking about funguses, talcum, vaccines,
waiting for the night to stand still
and for repentant fingers to become firmer.

When you look in the mirror, what you don't see is
the farce of pity
and contrition.
I'm so tired, dog.
Don't turn on anything, switch off
the scalpel lamp, peace,
your customary visor. The lapel of my coat
buried by fire.

On the polder with the director of dunes
the storm gathers. A bay horse at rest.
That river bend at nightfall.

Only he remained; and the open corridor.
It was already morning. When he turned around
I saw him facing the dock, the ship
advancing toward the other night,
his eyes speckled by the foliage.
And he waved and smiled. Drowning.

When they arrived, the landscape had already disappeared.
They drew the blinds, no one would hear them call.
The fire had opened the body's stronghold
in the slaughterhouse of another embrace.

Leaning silently over the railing
he found the moonlight again; he saw under the canal
the satiny light, the place that had been a house,
a negative of the stone,
a photo in duplicate multiplied by three.

As I walked, the day darkened;
it was at night that I met you.
You, the bird-catcher. In the gray
between high-tension wires; and the crane;
and the chiseled rainbow
phantom of beams.

In the high-backed black wooden chair
lay your coat. It wafted over the furniture
its fevered aroma
where before you arrived I often hid
my face that seemed to swell with castration.

Turning around for the farewell
I found the tears that made my eyelids
sand, in a mockery of the time that was ending.
Worse. In the certainty that the time was ending with
yet more time to suffer the time,
the devastation of waiting for the end.

When the letters arrive (across a different border,
behind which we've already been forgotten

by the one who remembered us
with these words from an earlier moment
when we were forgetting him), a vitriol caresses
the retina that had slowly lost affection.
You said I'd gone away without letting you know.
And I thought you were the one who'd left.
Delusions, a useless cloud charged with water that falls
in another place, inhospitable but real.

On seeing its definitively immobile face,
its blood all coagulated, a crumbling stone,
will that frightful object
still be the body for which we wept,
to which we brought the final teacup, the final
pill, the final terrified smile?
Something tells us that it is altogether
different; that nothing is there; that this is not
what we're grieving for.

We discover that all that there was has departed.
And what was it? Is the body then the soul?
The bursting of arteries the ultimate belief?

Pitchers of brass and of Frisian clay,
two nails securing a braid of onions,
the coffee grinder on the ledge
of the stairs leading up to the patio,
a film of flour covering the floor.
Your mother's forehead was exposed,
her hair pulled back. In the photograph.
At a round table covered with tow cloth
her right hand held the bread as her left
poured the mug of milk into a large
bowl. The sugar, eggs and jam
were in the middle of the table; and in a playpen,
with a toy in hand and hair almost white
in the yellowed light, sat you
with your crying mouth still milky,
your lips still unformed.

Nearly all the facades, except the one where I knocked,
had a door in the middle with glass
toward the top and, on either side, a narrow row
of three windows set higher than street level.
Above this was another floor with fewer,
narrower windows and no shutters.
And perched on the armament of darkened brick
was one last room with a broad window
over which the quasi-hexagonal roof came together.
From there a luminous stream issued forth
as I walked down the street to call you.

It ended in a wall of iron bars, containing the tide
of remaining foliage, likewise ready to fall.
The man who sold me so many flowers
took shelter next to the barrel organ.
Behind the plate glass window I leaned
and saw the maple, the poplar and the ash,
and it was then that I heard you arrive,
a Dutch boy leading a bicycle by the hand.

Amid the soft noise and haze of cigarettes
and of everything else with which the civil
indifference of those of the night encircled us
we shared the secret that gave
more gist to our reencounter,
calling us to a quietude that kissed
the very air separating our lips.

The imposing wall of the station, the terminal
ruins behind it, another abandoned train,
the river hemmed by cement shores,
the warehouses, stone crushers, a Chinese pavilion.
Then the canal. Not the congenial artifice
bordered by a street whose houses acquire
a haunted charm. Nor a furrow that divides
green lots overlying the black earth.
But one already tense with the throbbing of the waves,
with a long line of mangled barges
hauling farm machinery and rubble.

Already with seamen who've learned how to ascend
to the blockade where the sea is suspended
over your country to which I say farewell.

We walked along the walls that rose above what wasn't there.
Enclosed in the dregs of high winds.
And barriers wafted in the battlements.
And we call desire a brief funeral:
that of the fear of becoming what we already are,
what we stubbornly hide and still remain.

It was so easy to talk with you during the journey
about the Dutch disaffection for their own language,
as if we all belonged
to some other country.
Without knowing or seeking it
I could almost hear
your thought not thinking
so that I could understand. Was this a way of loving?

Language that never grew, calvinized
in the monopoly of the best product, on a route
with scant territory and few colonists;
an easily defended fortress and a couple of buildings
for the records, storage of goods, personnel;
and nothing to do with the locals, just an unequal exchange.
And that's what you'd like, near-exclusive rights
over two natives from the south – of your color,
unfortunately.
And you sit in a sea-colored suit
at the desk, the scar,
the magnet of the multinational.

Without a past of apparitions and saints,
without their images and banners,
without the incense of ritual costumes
with drums, timpani, and trumpets
in processions wending through villages,
your body's soul has a different neurosis,
burning at anchor for an encounter.

The commercial campaign wasn't enough;
the cross that wounds was also necessary,
the will not to have but to destroy.

The shout pushed away the covering hand
in the inertia of a schematism and I called.
A corner where turrets opened the dark
of lightning and the false denial and I called.
The distended skin almost answered
from the moat, from the cistern, from all infected places.
The night took the shape of your body, bloated,
gutted, with few stars attending
the burial march of clouds over the tramway,
the freighter, the motorboat, the container truck.

I didn't want to speak of that canal. I walked on,
flanked by catapults, round iron balls,
and the rest of the technicolor material of old films;
all that was missing were people. There was I, shouting
past the visible glory of the flagstones, past
the atrium where soldiers spent the night, past
the stables and the neighs that did not still my voice.
Only I was in the garrison. Surrounded
by the narrow streets, the market, the secret
bustle of goods that you crossed
with a whistle, pitting against the birds and sky
an indifference on its way to someone.
You would never see the old wall, the broken yellow,
the ideal height of the cathedral carried off by a gale.

It must be hard for someone lying
in the rest of the autumn I lived
not to feel in my lips' fleeting pressure
and in the unusual haste of my ejaculation
that your image accompanied me every day
in all the places and all
the encounters that made up the trip.
There's a certain delirium in being possessed
by a body with whom I exchanged nothing
except in the faraway region of dialogues

and in the indecisive hypotheses of youth
when still indifferent to pain. Still confident
in the falseness of passions that can be conceived
with words in a café. Still liable to catechisms.
There was a young man's head so blond
it was magenta, with silica eyebrows
and a fierce neck charging into the depths
of an indecipherable land.

My arms must have been different when they let go
of the other arms that sought me
but no doubt understood, without knowing what.
They no doubt accepted this and no doubt closed up
in that place within where we will not allow
a little, too little, of another to destroy us.

The mortal air of houses grows
in the sadness after nonintercourse.
The clouds rush by, taking pigeons with them,
and pointed slate rooftops shatter
into radiations of darkness in the trapped water.

We had talked about everything the night before,
about the suffocation, about picking up later,
but I didn't think it would happen.
With my throat the opposite of Holland,
dry, unable to talk.

I saw the chart of the company's blood.
In the flourishing of sales, the line dangled
exchange rates of oil over my head.
As the telefax sounded, a screen of numbers
was now your face.

Your hands hesitated over my sweater,
lost again in their fear of clinging
to the miraculously woven metal of saliva.
They were hands that didn't know how to grasp.

What I have learned is this: to dub as nonlove
the emotion that doesn't understand what it wants,
confounding feelings in an aridness so heavy
I can't begin to fathom how a plane can fly
in this endlessness of sky that brings the end.

But it ended hours earlier. Night
was coming on, the hotel growing dark, and
our hands clung a long time. All that time,
no time at all.

Translated from Portuguese by Richard Zenith

Terje Holtet

LARSEN

Unfortunate Canoe Quotes

It was of course her idea. I sat there the best I could, mainly in awe of the speed we reached without either of us rowing especially hard, just as occupied with holding my balance as paddling. It seemed we had more than enough on our hands just following our own movements, but I had also never sat in a canoe before. I sensed how one slight movement could tip the canoe over, it felt so anyway, and noticed the weight of my body in a completely different way; my center rose and made my head seem like a lead weight, as if somehow condensed. On the whole, sitting in the middle of a river in that way made it impossible to concentrate on anything other than not turning over, impossible to think about anything other than maintaining speed, not losing balance.

But as I said, it was my wife's idea, she was the one who had gotten it into her head that we would spend a weekend together in this way, just the two of us in a canoe upriver as far as we can go, she had said, we can make it back in about an afternoon, just following the sluggish current downstream. There has to be a first time, she said, you can't just sit inside with your head and thoughts buried in a book.

I let her interpret my silence as a sign that I had let myself be persuaded by her irrefutable arguments. It was just as well that she understood that this was new to me and had already emphasized that we were going to take it easy, that the trip was exactly suited for a beginner and that she would show me how one behaved in a canoe, how one should sit, hold a paddle, and keep a steady course. That's why I was a little surprised when she sat in the front and placed me in the back, since I figured that she of course would sit in the back, the natural place for the one who was going to control the situation. Watch how I do it, she said, and began to paddle with accustomed movements, and it soon became apparent that it was as easy as she'd said it was.

I have to admit that I could feel something of the special stillness and calm that everyone talks about when they gladly tell of their experiences with nature, when they bring up at every opportunity the special stillness which makes you realize something of the silent woods' superior eternal immobility, just then I could understand the meaning of such stories. Yet I knew that the purpose of this trip lay somewhere else.

One may say what one will, but such alleged whims always have a motive. The whole thing is so completely visible on her there, sitting in the other half of the canoe, with her back against me, of course, that apparent calm, something definitely weighing on her, and I knowing what it must be.

If the weather holds, she will get a beautiful brown color by the end of the day. Some spots of the white suntan lotion she has rubbed on herself can be seen on her shoulder blades. They move with her muscles under her soft skin.

I say that I love her.

She paddles.

I say that I am going to tell it like it is, no detours, no paraphrasing, but right to the point. I say here you have the naked truth, exactly as it was, nothing more and nothing less.

I tell her I sat alone at a table at the Café Tehola, a great place to spend the evening because nothing ever happens there, you know the kind, and I wanted nothing other than to be left in peace, when she suddenly stood before my table, came right up to me. It seemed I could feel her whole body against my leg, she said hello and I answered her. She asked if I didn't know who she was. I decided to tell her that I unfortunately had to admit that I didn't. She said Agnes. I said hello Agnes. She said Agnes B. "Unfortunately" was something I had said to be polite, I'm certain about that, I could of course have just said, "No, I don't," but I knew who she was. Or I could have said, "So, it's you is it," that I read her book reviews with great interest and was happy that there were still people in the dailies who were able to combine insight and understanding with enthusiasm, and had the ability to formulate both enthusiasm and critique with credibility intact, or something like that. Instead, I asked if she wanted something, a glass of wine, a drink, whatever, and she nodded, looked at my glass and said she would gladly have some red wine also, dark red wine, so I ordered a glass of red wine for her. Should we share a bottle instead, she then said, and I waved the waiter back to the table and changed my order. He was not in the least irritated by that. She thought that we two had something in common in this multitude of lowbrows. I made a note of that expression.

My wife paddles and says that that was not much of a rejection, something I admit she's right about, but I thought of adding that I, as opposed to her, was not especially rejecting by nature, but kept things inside. It would not have made her less hostile, I realize, but would have instead made her pain worse, and there was no reason to wish for a development in that direction.

I wasn't the one who put things on this track, I mean, I was, but it wasn't I who laid out this strange form of settlement. The worst is that I know that she'll never believe me if I tell her the truth, she'll never believe me again, for she wants me to be reduced forever to a pitiful liar, someone she'd never again be able to trust, never have faith in.

I say that Agnes B said she was a literary critic. I explain that despite everything she had earned a kind of apology, an explanation for why I didn't recognize her name. The waiter came rather quickly with a bottle and two new glasses. I let her taste the wine while I emptied my glass, which I had actually managed to draw out a good while. The waiter then filled both of the two new glasses, took the one I had emptied, and disappeared with waiterlike movements. I had not noticed him earlier that evening, he really was a proper waiter, carried himself the way real waiters often do.

My wife asks why I was so occupied with the waiter, something I can't give a satisfactory answer to.

You know how I am, I try, but then I give up, she already doesn't want to understand, or more accurately, she wants to understand all too well. Not that that stuff about the waiter was so important, but she'd already seen through my wretchedness, to put it mildly – just the word that she probably would have used – the attempt to lead her attention to the waiter's movements, and I have to admit that the waiter's movements were entirely insignificant.

My wife looks straight ahead, upriver, but I know that she feels my movements. I feel clearly watched, which I don't like at all. I have always experienced being watched as uncomfortable, there is just something similar about it to stage fright, limelight paranoia, as opposed to the waiter who is glad to be seen, who wishes to be watched, noticed, to awaken hushed attention, and who in some situations is almost certainly stimulated by all the hungry eyes, in a double sense, which follow him.

"You're not paddling," my wife says, still not turning around.

"I'm listening," she says.

"Please continue," she says, "if there is something you want to tell me."

I say her hair was long and dark, and she had thick bangs which lay completely down in her eyes. Her hair and masculine mouth gave her an Oriental look, but I sat there with the feeling that she too readily strove for such an impression, and thereby lacked the subtlety to succeed in her attempt to seem dangerous.
I don't want to go so far as to say that she failed, I'd rather say that her estimated abilities were probably not completely up to par and that she had let slip between her fingers some small, though no less revealing, details. Her lipstick, for example, badly chosen, too red for the shape of her small lips. With the extremely red lipstick her mouth became a cut in her face, a fresh and bloody razorblade cut in her pale skin.

Her mouth moved the whole time, and I remember that I for one short moment almost delighted in that somewhat painful, almost revolting feeling of staring into living bloody muscle tissue.

My wife says nothing, but I hear how she groans with impatience in the front of the canoe. And so, she thinks, when is he going to get on with it. But she can't complain about me not paddling my best, and anyway this was her idea, not mine.

I say so we sat there with our wine glasses. I noticed that, actually, I'd had enough to drink, I had decided to get up early the next morning to continue the work on my manuscript which had lain waiting so long and which I unwillingly have to admit still sat deep inside me. I had in other words mostly needed a long and proper workday, but I remained seated and conversed with this, what should I call her, this almost desperately Oriental woman, yes, because that was what she was, that is the only way to describe her, although it possibly sounds a little violent, I simply couldn't come up with any other description, I remained seated and conversed with this almost desperately Oriental woman who sat at my table and drank wine, somewhat against my wishes, because my intoxication would maybe have made it possible to sleep if I went home then, I felt it, sleeplessness would maybe have let go for a few night hours. But I didn't go home, I remained seated. As did Agnes B.

She said it was funny that she bumped into me just that evening, she had actually just read my debut novel again. She said that what first fascinated her was the underlining desire which lay between the lines, that underlying desire which gave my texts a special intensity. It was that intensity she found so interesting. I nodded and said, I admit, what one should say when a literary critic says such things, namely that it was a very observant and therefore interesting reading. She leaned forward and said that that desire in my text found a completely singular sounding board in her own desire. She explained that men were often afraid of that desire, that they felt threatened by her passion. She said men found her to be an extremely demanding and progressive lover. She said she demanded that men give her everything because she herself gave absolutely everything, and that often scared them. Then she asked if I were the kind of man that allowed himself to be frightened by a woman's desires. She said she thought not.

I was formulating an answer when she said she liked men who didn't talk too much. She said two sensitive minds could communicate in other ways. So I decided to keep quiet, and leaned back in my chair instead.

My wife waits. Paddles and waits. Certain that she knows what I'm trying to tell her, and this absolute certainty is more than enough. If it just weren't for this absolute certainty of hers. Once I asked her to look away when I had to take a pee. It was an embarrassing scene. She asked what I meant by it, something I of course couldn't answer, while at the same time I became uncertain whether she really didn't understand my point. I told her to forget it. It ended of course with her locking herself in the bedroom. I tried in vain to get her to let me in. I said I didn't want to spend the night on the couch in my own house. I said she could pack up and go home. You can sleep in the toilet, she said then.

But still, here we sit, I thought, man and woman, she three years younger than I. Friends react to the fact that I call her my woman. Why not say wife? I've never been able to give them an answer, just as they've never been able to understand why we live separately and not together, how we could marry without moving in together, why we decided at all to get married, was it that we didn't want to live together or just couldn't? I don't know, it just feels more natural to call her my woman, and when one is born with an appearance that went out of fashion forty years earlier, it's just what one becomes, everything one does ends up out of step. It awakens suspicions in people, they are too ready to think that you do it to make yourself interesting, like the waiters and their waiter movements.

There is the last century in everything about you, someone once said, a person I think of as a good friend. I understood it as her trying to give me a sort of cultural pessimism, and I defended myself as best I could with the argument that I to the best of my ability always tried to give a setting and a content that was possible to live with, and that I felt in no way threatened by all those who tried to characterize me as an unconscious aesthete.

I say when we had emptied the bottle, Agnes B asked if we should go to her house and drink a little more there. She said she actually hated these small smoke-filled cafés. She said it was impossible to talk together in a place like this. I was a little surprised because the comment didn't seem to go with the other things she'd said.

"A little surprised," my wife says, without stopping her even paddling. She has found a rhythm now, her balance is perfect, she apparently doesn't need to exert herself in any way.

"Did you say a little surprised?"

"Yes," I say.

This woman suggested that we take a taxi to her house and end the evening there with a drink. I thought it was just as well since it had become late, the next day was already spoiled. And she had also begun to make me a little curious.

My wife paddles. Silence. Waiting. She has a strong back. I am also paddling. No, I have no problems with understanding my wife's suspicions, in that way they are justified.

"Your back is beautiful," I say.

She paddles.

I say I said that I would tell it like it is, right? And I tell it exactly like it is.

I say it was when we first sat in the cab that I noticed her perfume. It had, as one could expect, an Oriental character, a rather aggressive thick strongly spiced fragrance, almost like soy, which of course must be completely the wrong association, no woman wants to smell like a kitchen regardless of how exotic it might be, but it was still soy I thought about, soy and a touch of garlic, everything other than a woman, everything other than an attractive seductress. Then the taxi driver asked her politely to put out her cigarette, he unfortunately did not allow smoking in his car. His voice was sterner when he had to repeat his request, and I for a moment was uncertain if she was going to ignore him, but she finally rolled down the window and tossed her cigarette out with a reluctant motion. She said it's just around the corner here, the next block on the right. I can't say if I particularly understood her actions. Neither the perfume or her actions. In general, she'd begun to bug me.

Of course I paid for the taxi. That was fine, the only thing was that I felt I almost accepted something, I didn't know what it was, to so obviously pay for the taxi as if at that moment a contract was signed of a type I wasn't sure I liked, she got out of the cab, I paid, something was confirmed with that, with that we'd pinned down how we wanted the whole thing to progress, the premise had been set.

I asked the driver for a receipt. I gave him what you could call a reasonable tip, and he asked me what date I wanted him to write on the receipt. While I was opening the door, he wished me good night, and good luck. That I paid for the wine was a different matter, I had invited her to sit at my table. On the other hand you could say that since I bought the wine it was only natural that I paid for the cab.

My wife says she thinks rather that Agnes B invited herself.

She may be right about that, but as long as we have separate budgets it has strictly speaking nothing to do with her. It was also Agnes B's apartment we were on our way to, her invitation was more of a counterbalance, a not necessarily so sensational way to round out the evening, and partly against my wishes since I realized that I at least should have had a little cold water and lain in my own bed by the open windows, but when the next workday was already spoiled I could just as well let things take their course, I had nothing to lose, one last drink at her place would just consummate the next day's misery.

Another side of it of course was that I didn't want to give Agnes B the impression that I was afraid of what she'd said about the kind of demands she made on her lovers, which, according to her, had been many. I would have in all probability made a pathetic figure of myself if I'd refused and said I had to go home, then she would have simply given me a contemptuous look and disappeared from the Café Tehola, where there were still a lot of people. At the door she would have turned around, looked at me with something like pity, then left with a haughty smirk on her small lips. I saw no reason to give her that upper hand, I understood that she was the type who would make use of such an upper hand at a later opportunity. The whole evening was put in place by her suggestion, that was what she wanted to arrive at, it was her game and she had finally reached the point where I could follow her or be humbled. I had, in other words, no choice, I had to follow her home for a last drink.

I say that her apartment makes a completely different impression than her perfume, naked white walls, sparsely furnished, steel pipes and black leather, the whole thing had an ascetic feel, rather different from what I had expected on the way up the stairs. I have to admit that that design suited her better than the one I'd imagined, but that didn't help.

We sat there side by side on her sofa, each with a drink. As a bartender it seemed she wanted to be spoken of as very generous with liquor and equally avaricious with ice cubes, something I obviously didn't mention. She was curious about what I was writing, and I told her a little about my idea for the novel, I felt I had to, told her about the lifeguard who tries again and again to describe the only swimmer that comes every day. I had to say something, but it seemed she was interested, she said she liked men who dared to write about the sexual forces between men. I didn't understand exactly what she meant by that, and to be honest, I didn't even understand how that could have been relevant to what I told her about my idea for the novel, as most of her comments on literature were irrelevant, as almost everything she so hastily blended together was meaningless, but I tried anyway to formulate some kind of answer, and then she interrupted me to say she wondered if I wasn't gay. I'm not going to say that her comment surprised me, on the contrary it seemed natural as an extension of her abrupt interpretation of what I had told her about my novel idea. Not just that she was getting quite drunk, she seemed increasingly more revolting to me, to say it right out. On the whole, when I saw her as she really was, I found her not in any way attractive, and it wasn't even possible to have a sensible conversation with her, everything became just allegations.

My wife paddles. She's strong, the canoe still glides at a good speed. I feel my shoulders getting sore from the unaccustomed movements.

"And then," she says.

I say I answered in a rather measured way that I wasn't gay and that it wasn't a gay novel that I was writing. I maybe should have said that such a question was too dumb for me to be able to answer, but I decided to be polite. I'm usually polite. If some see it as a weakness, I don't care. Then Agnes B asked if I was afraid of the woman inside me. I couldn't think of anything to parry with other than asking which one of them she was talking about. She got up and went into her bedroom. I hadn't even had half the drink she'd served me. I remained seated. I lit a cigarette.

"And then," she says.

I say that two cigarettes later I was still sitting alone on the sofa and I understood that I'd managed to get rid of her. She did not have a single plant, the only possibility I had to get rid of my drink was to drink it. It went slowly, but I had plenty of time, she had fallen asleep, I called for a cab, but when the woman on the other end asked for the address, I realized that I was not quite sure of where I was, so I just hung up. This also was not such a problem. I found one pretty quickly. Half an hour later I could finally go to bed. Alone.

My wife paddles. I don't know if I've managed to give her an explanation that she can accept, but I have anyway given her a story, she has gotten the story she asked for by taking me out in this canoe, just the two of us, she has no reason to complain, what more could she want?

I could of course add how Agnes B came into the room again, how her naked body came toward me, but that's not a good solution, we'd both had too much to drink and the next morning I left pretty early, in pretty bad shape. And as long as I don't tell her about my other meeting with Agnes B then everything can continue. It's a question of making choices, and letting a life together with my wife continue is a choice,

I thought. So I have at the same time chosen not to tell her about my other meeting with Agnes B. It's a choice. And Agnes B no longer means anything. That was also a choice.

It was exactly then that the canoe almost tipped over, it was my fault, I wasn't concentrating, the oar slipped and I almost tipped over to the right. In a glimpse I saw the canoe tip over, I saw us go under, saw myself grab onto her strong shoulders. Only her quick reaction saved us, she recovered balance for us both so rapidly that either it must have been pure reflex or else she was just waiting for something like that to happen.

"That was damn close," I said.

The laughter comes, also a reaction, but how strange and artificially merry it seems. My wife turns around. It strikes me that I see her face for the first time this whole afternoon, her face, the only face I'm capable of seeing even with my eyes closed. She smiles. Water drips from the paddle.

"Thanks," she says.

A few more strokes, then I also rest my paddle.

"Thanks for telling me the truth," she says.

She says I still surprise her. I tell her I'm that kind of guy. What else could I say?

She paddles. She is beautiful. She's all I have. It is she who gives me the feeling of being alive. Without her I'm nothing, I would know nothing. One day I'll tell her that.

Translated from Norwegian by Krister Swartz

MIRA *Magen*

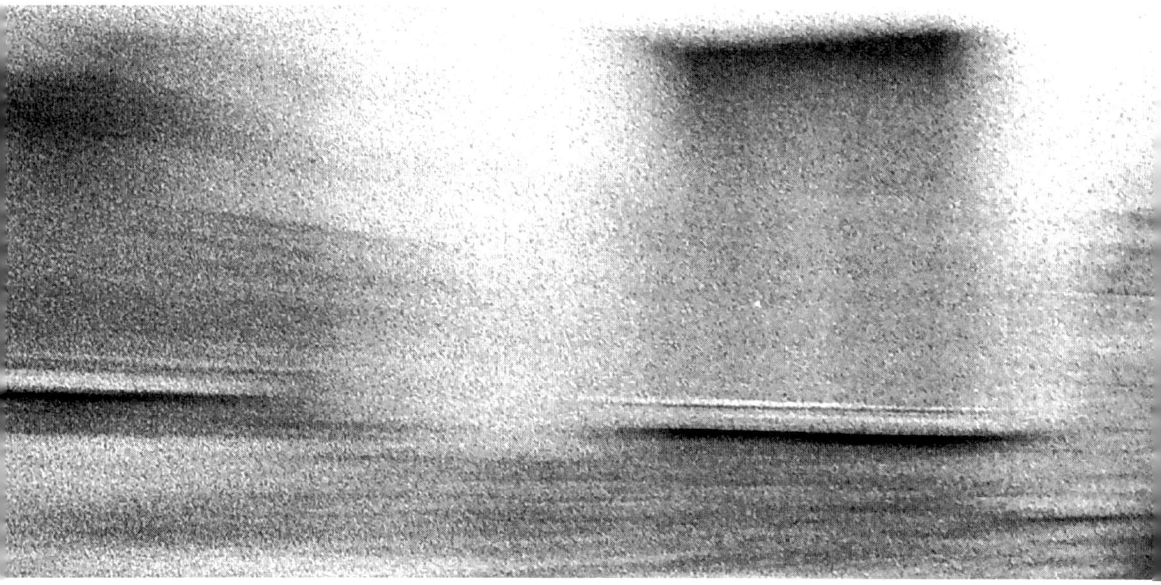

The Red Dress

Sometimes the sky here is like the downy feathers of little chicks, flying high, and the more you want it to be lower and closer to you, the higher it soars, and the more you stretch your fingers and shout until your vocal cords burst, the sky is like the downy feathers of little chicks, weightless.

Mother will serve tea soon. Two saccharin tablets will shoot up spinning and fizzing to the top of Malkale's cup, her sugar has been high lately. Of course, she can live on lettuce and boiled string beans, but when it comes to swollen sizzling apples on pie crust, she prefers an extra injection of insulin in her thigh to a nervous and disappointed stomach. They drink tea before or after harsh words, never during. Soon they'll finish talking, well, Mother has actually been finished for awhile, she's silent, but even though Malkale Cooperstock is inhaling the hot cinnamon smell, mouth watering, she's restraining herself because she still has things to say and she left everything in the middle so she could come and say them.

You know, she's past her prime for a girl, she says to Mother, and I don't have to tell you that overripe apricots fall to the ground and rot.

The light outside is strong, a good light for choosing material for a dress. At Marcel's store they're taking the fabrics out into the sun now, because only in the sunlight can you tell the difference between olive-green and bottle-green. Sammy drags out bolt after bolt and Marcel arranges them by color. I would gladly sew something summery in a soft viscose, but so many things have been said about me here that the words bunch up on each other, creating a fence between me and the fabrics. For years I've been walking on the other side of the street, seeing the fabrics only from afar, and sometimes something shines from inside the store, maybe the glitter of Sammy's chain, or maybe the sparkle in his eye, I don't know, and I don't stop to find out.

In the middle of cooking, Malkale had buttoned her thin wool coat over her house dress and walked three short blocks to come talk to Mother. She doesn't leave her house without that coat until the end of May. I'm in my room, and if it wasn't for the young goldfinches chattering on the branches of the plum tree, I would hear every word. Even without seeing Malkale I know that she hasn't unbuttoned her coat yet, with its smell of fresh crushed garlic and jellied chicken feet trapped in the lining from the heavy pots she presses up against her house dress to move them from the counter to the stove, from the hem she uses as a glove to handle the red-hot frying pan or drain the noodles. All day long she looks out the window over the sink, squinting to see between the drops of oil spattered and stuck on the glass, watching the fields of blue lupine that extend beyond the yard. This season the blue is as vivid as the blue of the hat she bought the year of Saul's bar mitzvah.

Ten years already, but people don't forget, Malkale says, it's stuck on your daughter like a birthmark. Even if she leaves and moves to the city, she won't be able to get rid of it, because words spread like wildfire.

Mother doesn't answer, maybe she's thinking about Rosie Klein, who has already married off her youngest daughter. On Rosh Hashana, there will be six feathers on Rosie's and her five daughters' hats, bending in the breeze blowing through the round windows of the synagogue. Only my head will be bare among all the women who have already reached a height of at least five-five.

Malkale is so crazy to marry off Saul that she's even willing to stop knowing what she knows about me. She tells Mother that a new hole must be made in his belt every week because everything just falls off him, because there's no happiness in him.

We were thirteen when he said show me what you have in your mouth, and I turned my face toward the sun and opened my mouth as wide as I could and showed him the small wire braces on my teeth. He was fascinated and tried to look farther down behind my teeth, bending and stretching his thin neck to stare into the black hole of my throat all the way to its pink center. Later, he picked some lupine and handed me three blue blossoms on their stems, and I noticed that his fingers were soft and white like mine and that they had forgotten to iron one of his sleeves which was wrinkled like the neck of a turtle, the other was smooth with a sharp fold along its length. The sky was the height of the raspberry bushes growing near the fence and brushed our cheeks. Saul skipped across the field like a grasshopper, bearing his joy like someone bearing a young bird. I pulled petals from the flowers, saying yes, no, yes, no, and I knew that when I grew up I would have a boyfriend with hands like nutshells, brown and hard.

The end of April. The house smells of onions fried in soybean oil even though the windows are wide open. Malkale unbuttons her coat. Mother says that soon it'll be summer, and Malkale says that soon there will be plums for jam and how time flies, another year, and then another. Mother starts to say something about the sudden khamsin that ripened the kumquats early, as if the conversation was a canal that could easily be diverted, trying so hard to avoid the subject of how quickly time passes. But Malkale won't waste a minute now, because lukewarm apples don't smell the same, and they have to get to that point while the pie is still steaming and the raisins are still swollen with heat. Later they'll cool off and collapse like burst bubbles.

I'm ready to forget what these eyes have seen, she says. I remember it like yesterday. There were six fresh radishes in the sink. I peeled one of them and looked out the window. Everything up to the fence was a kind of bluish-purple color as if someone had spilled ink on the field, and all of a sudden your daughter, she was only fifteen...

Malka, not again, Mother says. She hasn't forgotten how I came into the house on that day wearing a dark red dress, my cheeks the color of pickled beets. Marcel had told me to come at noon to pick out material because sunlight shows true colors and neon lies. We walked out of her shop onto the dirt road in front of the grocery. She held big bolts of cloth up against me, and Sammy held a mirror in front of me. A blinding circle of white light escaped from the mirror and danced on the grocery walls. The dark red is the best, it makes you look like an actress, he said, returning the fabrics to the shop, the sun igniting a small fire on the golden circle dangling from his neck and releasing white sparks from his pinkie ring. He sat on a bolt of pink satin, moving his head back and forth to the music on the radio and spitting the shells of salted pumpkin seeds into the garbage. Marcel placed a tape measure around my waist and wrote in her notebook, then she placed it around my hips and wrote, and then from my shoulder to my waist, and finally she encircled my chest with it, but she only needed a small section, most of it just dangling in the air. Sammy bent to look at the numbers written in the notebook and said you should eat more, a man has to have something to grab onto.

Only very few people in our farm community wore pants as short as his. His legs were brown and hard against the pink satin, and his fingers looked like big peanuts moving to the rhythm of the song on the radio. I had never seen Saul's legs because he always wore long pants with shoes and socks. Malkale stuffs him with so many jellied chicken feet that I once dreamed his toes were covered with chicken skin.

All the windows are open, the leaves of the plum tree are fluttering, the wind ruffles the goldfinches' feathers, and still it's stuffy. There's no air, and the smell coming from Malkale's house dress is spreading through the rooms. Mother says enough Malka, enough of this already, and pushes the button on the electric kettle. But Malkale Cooperstock did not turn off the gas in the middle of the day and walk three short blocks just for apple pie.

Your daughter is hard and closed like an olive pit, she says, and Mother doesn't say a word. She too saw Saul's face redden like an open rose when we walked past him last Saturday. He greeted us, his eyes looking down at the pebbles that had been scattered on the road near the synagogue, and I couldn't do anything about how the sun made my hair look golden, or how the wind blew it around my shoulders and made turquoise-colored waves on the pretty dress I was wearing.

It really could work. He's serious and responsible and she's a smart cookie, you can't put anything over on her, says Malkale. They called me Cohen's little tramp when it happened, but since then the wedding canopy has been folded up and stored away in the synagogue, and all the spring chickens have been married off already, and Saul is still single, and he blushes every time he sees me, Malkale brings Mother plum jam and always greets us with the kind of serious and weighty *hello* usually reserved for the neighborhood doctor.

The dress was clear, deep, dark red, the color of ritual wine. Marcel spread it out on the counter and said that I would look like a princess in it, and the whole store was filled with a red glow from the fabric, even Sammy's eyes were like buttons of blood. Marcel placed one sleeve on the other and folded the dress lengthwise, pinning a note on it saying how much we had already paid and how much we still owed, and Sammy said a person could go crazy from the smell of material all day long, and he walked out of the store after me. The light outside was the way it is now, the kind that makes the leaves transparent and the houses look as if they have been bathed in milk. Sammy's legs were golden brown against the yellow gravel.

So listen, Malkale says, I'm peeling the radishes, and all of a sudden I see your daughter wearing her blue school dress disappear into the raspberry bushes with that character. Mother breaks into a spasm of small coughs, tapping her feet on the floor, each in a different rhythm, and Malkale waits patiently for Mother's coughing to subside so she can continue her story. They come out of the bushes fifteen minutes later and all of a sudden her dress is red, such a dark red color that all the blue flowers looked pale next to it, I was so upset that the radish fell right out of my hands. The switch on the electric kettle clicks, Mother opens and closes the oven noisily and coughs, but Malkale doesn't wait for the coughing to stop before she asks how could you let her wear red? She says she's amazed that Mother let me wave a red flag in front of a bull... Mother slices the pie, and the banging of the knife on the glass dish cuts through Malkale's words, and I can't hear what she says or how Mother answers her. Even now, in the oppressive air and after so many years, I can still smell the raspberries. I stood among the leaves and saw Cooperstock's forehead moving behind her window, pressing up against it and then disappearing.

Sammy says I'm dying to see you in that dress, you don't see a fifteen-year-old girl wearing dark red every day. Long spikes of wheat grew near the raspberry bushes, and the black tassels growing out of their golden florets brushed against Sammy's legs. He put his pinkie, the one with the ring, into one of the beards, and the bristles left scratches on it, and I took off my blue dress and put it down on the raspberry bush and very carefully took the new dark red dress out of its bag. The thin black tassels brushed against my naked shoulders, and he said I've never seen such white skin, and he helped me pull up the zipper ever so carefully from my waist to my neck, and I let him tie the belt in the back and the collar bow in front.

Marcel is right, a princess, he said, and I pursed my lips and twirled around like a model, and the dress caught on some thorns. When I stepped out from behind the bushes, the bill was still pinned to the hem of the dress, but it was crumpled and torn across the line showing how much we had already paid. Mother asked if I had gone crazy and said leave it for the holidays, who wears such an expensive dress in the middle of the week? Her eyes went wide and her mouth fell open, she was amazed at how well the dark red suited me, it's too beautiful, she said, and her mouth stayed open, and my face burned as if the dress was on fire.

Later on, they called me Cohen's little tramp, and the air became suffocating, like in the chicken coops after the chicken feed has been distributed, and the space between the houses seemed to shrink, and the distance between the roofs and the sky seemed to have expanded. The dark red dress remained as it was for all of these years, it's only people who experience things and change from minute to minute, from hour to hour. Fabric stays the same. The light from the window illuminates the material, and the leaves of the plum tree weave delicate lacy shadows on it. I can barely close the zipper now, the dress stretches almost to the bursting point across my chest, squeezes my waist, and reaches only to a spot above my knees. I take a wide turn around the room, like I did then among the spikes of wheat.

Malkale bends over the pie and says *oy vey* because of the sugar, and after the second *oy vey* she stops and asks why all of a sudden the kitchen looks so red and why the tiles look like Santa Rosa plums. She stops sucking the cinnamon off the apples, turns around and sees my long legs at the door and the dark red fabric ballooning out above my knees touching both sides of the door frame.

Take a piece for Saul, I tell her, picking up the largest slice to put in a plastic bag for him. A raisin falls and rolls onto her coat, coming to a stop on her knee, where it sticks like a beauty mark. Malkale Cooperstock doesn't move her knee, as if the raisin was a butterfly she didn't want to startle. Ever so slowly, she extends two fingers to pick up the raisin and gently places it whole and still swollen with heat into the bag which holds the cake for Saul, then closes it tightly, tying it with a double knot.

Translated from Hebrew by Sondra Silverston

Stephan *EIBEL*

For a painter it would be better not to be married. For a drinker, which he could perhaps become, it would be better to be married. A painter paints. A painter has to paint. That is linguistically and socially completely *logical*. A drinker drinks. A drinker has to drink. That is linguistically correct. If a drinker doesn't drink, it is linguistically correct, but socially not *logical*.

He just wanted to have a profession, and to devote himself entirely to his profession.

As a drinker he would have only one task: To be drunk. Drunk to the point of falling over.

He could become a drinker who didn't fall over. Maybe then his color psychologist friend and his former wife and current acquaintances would say: "I've never seen him fall over!" He would have a task that would require his complete attentiveness: Just don't fall over.

Icy streets, frosty, and he's not allowed to fall over. Again he would have survived a winter without having *fallen over*, he could have said to himself, not without pride. Walking tall, he ruminated, distancing himself from Stock im Eisen Square.

A politician drinks for his conscience. A writer for the inspiration. A worker drinks for professional reasons. But why does a drinker drink?

A drinker has to drink. So that he can be a drinker and have a duty to fulfill. A drinker's head often buzzes, and Fenster Helmut's head was already buzzing. When a drinker walks too quickly along the canal on a hot summer day, the alcohol comes out of all of the pores of his drinker skin.

The disadvantage of being a drinker was the constant comments from other people. Everyone knew something about drinking. One person would give advice about hangovers, another would say that you should only drink French red wines, the next only got drunk on Saturdays.

He wanted to be a real drinker, one who could drink without being criticized. An expert drinker.

Key in hand, he searched for the keyhole to the apartment. An average drinker might not find the keyhole to his apartment. An expert drinker, the drinker of all drinkers, always finds the keyhole. It becomes clear to the drinker in the course of his drinker time, of his drinker life, that finding the keyhole or not doesn't matter. Keyholes don't matter at all to a drinker. Partly because everyone else opens the door for a drinker, and partly because a drinker never opens any barred doors. As he flew over the threshold into the apartment, managing to support himself with his right hand, he resolved to postpone the difficult decision of whether to become a drinker starting today until tomorrow. If upon entering professional life, you fall into the entryway of the apartment, it must be obvious that a professional drinker's life would carry serious consequences.

"A profession isn't child's play," his father often said. He very carefully stood up, feeling a burning in his asshole that made *hearing and seeing* nearly escape him. Ultimately, the drinker's profession doesn't bring only unpleasant things with it, but also pleasant things, which Fenster Helmut noticed as he slammed the door shut.

He went into his room and noticed, despite his drunkenness, that the air was stuffy.

For the sake of appearances, he had set up four paint jars in his room. As a painter he had to have something to do with paints, said his color psychologist, which was also what he'd learned in school. He picked up one jar after another and put it down again. He took a swig of red from a jar. Fenster Helmut could barely breathe. He went into his wife's room. The paint didn't taste half bad. He turned the radio so that he could hear the music. He let the music become noise. The neighbor beneath him was dead. The neighbors on the other side of his wife's room hadn't yet moved in. Fenster Helmut didn't feel any tingling despite the red paint, despite the noise, no lessening of his horrendous headache. He didn't need to have sympathy with the neighbors' lives, which in any case didn't matter to him at the moment.

At times he had seen his wife in her room. He sat at her desk. So the important books came into being here. If he had a picture of this room and his wife, who smoked and wrote, this picture would need a frame. It was the only possible picture of his wife. And his wife couldn't have really shown this picture of how she smoked and wrote and gazed at the void in the piece of paper rolled into the typewriter. Her whole life she has wanted to be in love, she said to him, and that's how I have to write. She always had something she could think about. In her youth she had been the fastest swimmer, so she knew swimming pool life. She had set up her life like a swimming pool. The edges of the big pool would contain hardworking officials and a great void. The audience sat on the seats far beyond the void. He was very similar to his wife's father. He hung out with the void at the edge of the pool.

No one could paint a picture of his wife in this room. A picture with a frame, maybe, but not a picture of his wife. She sat there and gazed at the blank paper. She lived, and pictures are dead.

He sat in the place that had probably become the most important place in her life. Looked from one corner to the next, stood up and turned the music down. The noise didn't leave him with a sense of freedom anymore, so he turned the radio all the way off.

A pair of pants lay on a chair and her nightgown lay in bed. His wife had never let him sleep in her room. His wife had painted two small windows on the wall. A "picture" was framed with his signature between the windows. The "picture" had been written in green paint, his signature clearly legible in red paint.

The writing "picture" was lively. The marks around the picture a cheap frame that fit. His signature was small but easy to read.

He lay down on his wife's bed. With both hands he drew an outline of her head and her body down to her toes. Comparing the outline with his own height, he determined that his wife was no taller than fifty centimeters. He didn't want to stand up and make her bigger, he had done so well putting her in a frame. Fenster Helmut felt increasingly nauseous. He went in his room and drank a swig from the jar of white paint. Finally his body had its way with him. Fenster Helmut didn't have his body under control in the least. While running to the toilet, he emptied a part of the contents of his stomach in his son's room. At last, having arrived in the toilet, he threw up the red paint. The white paint hadn't hurt him, Fenster Helmut noticed, because he hadn't thrown it up. He screamed into the toilet bowl, "ä, ü, o," which would have been clearly understood in the pub. Here in the toilet there was no one who could understand anything, and in this situation Fenster Helmut didn't attach the least importance to even a bit of understanding.

Finally it got better. He flushed water in the toilet bowl, which made part of his vomit disappear. The red paint wouldn't flush away, which didn't matter to him anyway. In the child's room, he nearly slipped on his vomit. Finally he was in his wife's bed again, and he looked at the painted window.

He closed his eyes and nothing moved. He was glad. As a youth he thought that throwing up together with his friends was a necessity. His wife explained the senselessness of it all, after they both threw up in the same toilet bowl, and sprayed each other. He had retained a positive attitude toward his own throwing up.

He continued to gaze at the window and saw a narrow path that led downhill. His legs were on the go-cart and his hands steered. It was a dirt path. Over the course of the years, gravel and asphalt came. The go-cart stayed.

The house that his grandmother lived in was four hundred meters away from the narrow downhill path. He gazed deep into the window but didn't see himself. He just felt small. Other children walked with him and pulled the go-cart up the narrow path. For days, he watched himself riding the go-cart in his wife's painted window.

The house stood on a hill and didn't fit the hill. You didn't see that the house didn't fit on the hill until you climbed the mountain opposite. From an airplane the house fits, because from high above you don't see the hill, as he remarked years ago on a flight.

His memory fit in this room. From the house you could see other houses below, and a street uniting each house too, a street that used to be a dirt road and then was paved. His grandmother and mother waved at the train from the house. His little sister was sitting in the train. She went on vacation and amazed everyone because she didn't get homesick.

The steam that the locomotive left visibly *black* in the air moved slowly near the house. The train went around a big curve and disappeared behind a mountain. In the afternoon a train came from the other direction. With less steam. The children frequently waved to the people inside the train. The children understood that the work was dangerous. They were familiar only with the work of workers.

Fenster Helmut gazed into the other window and watched the worker repair a cylinder. The cylinder rolled and hamburgered the worker. "You're stupid," screamed one worker to the other, and, guilt-ridden, they acted like nothing had happened.

The wife of the hamburger was from Dresden. The young pretty woman considered an Austrian worker a capitalist. The capitalists are rich people who light cigarettes with paper money. The young woman was a kindergarten teacher and had an apartment in her hometown. The wife of the heretofore hamburger came to the capitalists' country, where the toilet was out in the hall. She had imagined it differently, said the young woman, but she still loves him, even if he's hamburgered.

His wife once wrote him a letter from Dresden. MY WORKPLACE MY BATTLEFIELD FOR PEACE, SOCIAL SECURITY THROUGH ECONOMIC GROWTH, she read on the banners. The many smokestacks poisoned the air. This memory didn't fit in a window. Herr Helmut Fenster lay in his wife's bed and breathed very loudly. The white paint had done him some good.

He had nothing to lose in his wife's room except all hope.

His world was his head, and the world no longer came out of his head. While laboriously cleaning off burnt-on food remains, he recognized that doing dishes was not his world. Looking, tingling was his world. He had to inflict the injury, the burn, not just because of the food remains, but also because of his world. Because of his tingling.

The slower Helmut Fenster seemed to himself, the faster his method of transportation had to become. At first, he had imagined going from one pension to the other on the tram, but now he would need the fastest spaceship to get far away, or very close.

For years they've both been in love. He was able to think of his *tingling* incessantly, and his wife wrote the books.

Nobody had to be alone.

He used to read books in order to fall in love with someone he could also lay aside.

In one of his wife's books that had been made into a film he recognized himself.

“I don’t like how you smell, how you put your feet on the table, how you’re dressed. You’re a megalomaniacal pusher. An oppressor. Don’t ask me anything else.”

He would have had to read the books to learn something about himself.

Fenster Helmut had the impression that writing was very important to his wife, but he didn’t know that she wrote because she wanted to express something.

He always thought that writing was an expression of her wish to be in love and didn’t think that she also wrote to state something about people.

His wife always expressed herself ironically about the writers’ club she was a member of. “The Author’s Club is meaningful because it’s confused with the Auto Club, and thus is world-renowned in Austria.”

“What’s progressive about the Author’s Club is that a moment of silence for late members truly lasts a moment.”

Maybe he had misunderstood.

Fenster Helmut ran to the toilet again. White paint trickled from his urine. He felt like a painter through and through as he sprayed his white urine into the red toilet bowl. It was a wonderful feeling for Fenster Helmut that no part of his body hurt.

He had never really gotten to know his body. He had a brain that thought. A head that had a face, and the remaining body, which did the widest variety of things independently, without him even having any idea what he was doing.

For years you live in your body and are glad when it trickles out of you. He shook his penis the way he shook men’s hands and lay down again in his wife’s bed.

He was supposed to understand his wife, and he didn’t even understand his body.

Maybe he should have said phrases to his wife which he’d heard from the countless guests in his studio, and which appeared intellectual.

Maybe he should have written down two such phrases daily and learned them by heart on the way home. During dinner he would have said the two phrases, and his wife would have thought she was married to an intellectual.

"Young talents die fast."

"A doctor wouldn't hang himself so quickly."

He even knew two phrases by heart, he remarked.

"A painter has to be archaic," his wife often said.

Had he said the intellectual-sounding phrases, they probably would have had to talk about them. Had he remained silent, he might have been considered archaic, but that was, "due to pedagogical reasons" – as his wife would have said – impossible.

He looked into his wife's painted window and couldn't find an answer.

He looked into the other window and saw the belt.

He saw a bridge, over which a tram drove. People stood under the bridge. They were waiting for the tram. Cars went back and forth, and pedestrians went forth and back. He saw movement and heard the noise that didn't come from the painted window but from the memory in his head. CAUTION AVALANCHES stood on the bridge.

Fenster Helmut couldn't look into the window anymore. He was very happy to be living in the inner city.

The child's room conveyed a sense of lots of noise and movement. He could definitely imagine painting a picture in the child's room.

His grandpa, he told the child, was a good soccer player. A goalie on the national team. He himself had played soccer well, but ever since his grandpa died, he had no longer played soccer. The child was very impressed by his lie. Fenster Helmut was an extraordinarily bad soccer player and was afraid to be forced to reveal his soccerplaying inability to the child. The child gazed at his greatgrandchildsoccerplayerlegs, and played soccer very well.

Maybe he should have strewn tacks in the crib as a prank. Have bought itching powder and strewn it in the child's underwear. But all of the good ideas came too late. "Adieu… I've found love," his wife wrote in the letter.

His situation was hopeless.

His child has gone away, his wife has gone away.

"Shall we go away?" his friend asked him in his youth, and that meant that they left the parental apartment for the open air. Whether open air meant the forest, the lake, the settlement, or, later, a bar, didn't matter at all. *Going away* meant going away from the parental apartment.

Many people told him: "We're going out on Saturday." He never figured out what *going out* meant. Thousands of people went out on Saturdays and he didn't know where they went. His wife went *away*. Away from him.

Once he went *out* with a friend of his wife and her husband. The friend's husband invited him to go out with them. They went to a restaurant. The food tasted good to him, he remembered, but he didn't dare ask where the two would go after dinner. He went home and waited to *go out*.

Now the taste of paint went away. Should he try green?

Green, like that primitive whore's meager clothing? If he had enough money, he would go to the primitive whore every day. He would even write a textbook to make the whore into his whore. A whore he was all-powerful to, and who did everything that he paid for. If he was a woman he would be a whore. A whore who let the men lick her tickler and pull her hair. A whore for masochists.

He would show the men. Ply them and screw them over and give them the impression that it was only *their* dick that was too small for him. No dick in the world would be big enough for his twat. No man too manly, no man a god. As a whore he would be a god himself.

He would have become a magnificent whore. He wouldn't get that new disease, either. As a whore he would break one dick after another. He would break all of the dicks in the world, and the disease would be done for.

How absurd that whores need a textbook. Masters wanted to be masters to be the master of life and death. Death is not allowed, and that's how you write a textbook, and that's why it's a dog's life. Fenster Helmut couldn't stand dogs. Five dogs, he could stand even less. If he had a dog or a cat he could be the master of life and death. "Who d'ya think y'are anyway?" the people asked him. If he had known, he would have answered.

He got up and went into his room. He drank a powerful swig of green paint. "Isn't he powerful," the people say, and he takes another powerful swig. "Isn't he powerful," the people say, and by that mean that *he* will one day die. Fenster Helmut carried the precious jars into his wife's room one by one.

Again he succeeded in *not* slipping on his vomit. He will mix the green paint with the black paint. He had drunk from all four jars. He still hadn't felt a tingle. He didn't want to smoke any cigarettes. First of all, he didn't know whether cigarette smoke and the enjoyment of paint were compatible, and secondly, he wanted to feel a tingle when he painted.

He painted and mixed the paints in his stomach. If he'd had a dog, he would have had it drink from the jar too.

He endured it like the President, who was an animal lover but didn't have a dog. If the President was in a bad mood, some people would kill themselves. If Fenster Helmut was in a bad mood, Fenster Helmut didn't necessarily notice it. "A bad president" is what the people say when the president isn't an animal lover.

Green and black weren't really compatible, Fenster Helmut noticed. To lessen his nausea he drank from the jar which contained white paint. Maybe the jar is still a quarter full, Fenster Helmut thought.

At the bank he had an account. The account showed thirty thousand points. Minus points.

Because the death sentence had been abolished, people had finally found a way to have themselves killed without being directly killed by a hangman. People's debts burdened them so much that they were killing themselves even when they had only a slightly less negative account balance. Fenster Helmut didn't have any problem with that.

He had grown up in the days when people still believed in money.

Those times taught him that the "Money God" was very unstable and needed a newer, more solid god behind Him, called the "Gold God" in the official jargon. In a pluralistic society, further gods were sought and found. "Uranium God," "Platinum God," whatever they were all called they couldn't impress Fenster Helmut because he was neither a technician nor a goldsmith nor a money printer.

He was a painter who prized the white paint above all, and again took a swig of it.

With a kilo of Gold God he could have gotten a great number of jars of white paint, but he didn't want to neglect the other paints, so as not to seem unfair.

Fenster Helmut sat in his wife's bed and saw a photograph. The photograph was near the painted window.

The young mother with the smiling child.

The young mother was his wife and the smiling child was his child. A child stays a child, even when this child one day becomes a father, Fenster Helmut considered, and a horrible thought suddenly occurred to him.

Immediately he downed the jar of white paint. He felt better and better. The white paint caused him to nod his head again and again. He had become a head nodder. Paint bewitches you, people say. Paint transforms you, Fenster Helmut ventured to say. If he were now to become a painter, he wouldn't have to burn his right hand like he did before. Wouldn't have to feel the terrible pain anymore. Red fit his thoughts. He took a powerful swig of red from the jar. Fenster Helmut figured his eyes were glowing. He could see the sparks that sprayed from his eyes. Hopefully the parquet floor wouldn't start to burn.

He looked into the window and saw a cart, not unlike the go-cart of his childhood, with a hidden teeny-tiny electric motor. The coffin was lying on it.

The coffin lay there importantly. The people walked behind the coffin. They walked up the hill behind the electric-powered cart. The people stopped at a shoveled-out pit. They formed a circle in which everyone faced straight ahead.

Like back in his childhood, he couldn't recognize himself in the window.

A holy man spoke of dust, which he knew meant radioactive dust. The holy man didn't speak for long, but the whole time with political allusions. A camion drove past the open pit along with a garbage truck from the city sanitation department. The holy man took a teeny-tiny shovel, a teeny-tiny scoop in his hand, and threw the scoop's contents into the open pit.

The coffin no longer lay on the electric-powered cart. He hadn't noticed where the coffin had gone. One by one the people facing straight ahead in the circle went toward the scoop, evoking admiration in Fenster Helmut. They had to take the scoop, and at the same time, with the same hand, they often slipped the man who gave it to them paper money.

The holy man was the only one who didn't trust his own adroitness.

Two women were the center of attention. Both dressed in black. One fell apart, the other, after she saw that, fell apart even more clearly. The people standing in the circle once again whispered in each other's ears. The color psychologist friend was clearly recognizable in this painted window.

Fenster Helmut didn't want to idly watch the events any longer. He drank from the jar of black paint. The people standing in the circle disbanded. The open pit remained there, alone.

Fenster Helmut felt bad. He felt bad like never before in his life. He drank the whole pot of black paint.

His wife was with him by mistake. His wife was with him because of his name. He was called Fenster Helmut. He was a painter. The painted windows led his wife to believe in *fate*. Only a painter named Fenster can be my husband, who I can be happy with, because Fenster means window, and my painted windows accompany *me* my whole life, in all apartments, in all places *I* have the painted windows with me. She must have thought that way and never known that he wasn't a painter.

He mixed the remaining paints in his stomach. One intensification of nausea after another overwhelmed him. Another jet of paint mixture came out of his mouth and made deep furrows in the painted windows. Fenster Helmut shook with cramps and felt a tingling that was not unpleasant. He was a painter who could feel tingling while painting. A painter with his entire body. He sprayed the paint mixture from his mouth all over the bed. His mouth was bursting with paint.

The painted window was now a window with deep grooves in the wall and a paint mixture of red, black, white, green.

Before, the window had been a painted place, but now it was a place that hadn't existed before.

Fenster Helmut couldn't think about *utopia* anymore. He felt only paints. He spewed a feeling of longing along with the color red in the direction of the desk. He spewed black in the direction of the doors, as well as additional paint mixtures. Soon he couldn't breathe anymore, and he had a horrible fear which in black he couldn't feel anymore. He threw up again. Brown came out of his mouth and devastated the red of longing, which had eaten into his wife's desk.

He tangled himself in his wife's sheets, he would never let go of the sheet in his right hand. He didn't feel his broken left arm anymore, and he was no longer afraid of another needed burn.

As adieu, black stayed in his head.

Fenster Helmut didn't forget anything he could reproach himself with. But had he looked around his studio, he would have been bothered by the fact that he hadn't destroyed his tingle experiments, his longing. Black didn't stay inside his head. His whole head was black.

Translated from German by Nancy Isenson

TOMAŽ

Šalamun

Lacquer

Destiny rolls over me. Sometimes like an egg. Sometimes
with its paws, slamming me into the slope. I shout. I take
my stand. I pledge all my juices. I shouldn't
do this. Destiny can snuff me out, I feel it now.

If destiny doesn't blow on our souls, we freeze
instantly. I spent days and days afraid
the sun wouldn't rise. That this was my last day.
I felt light sliding from my hands, and if I didn't

have enough quarters in my pocket, and Metka's voice
were not sweet enough and kind and solid and
real, my soul would escape from my body, as one day

it will. With death you have to be kind.
Home is where we're from. Everything in a moist dumpling.
We live only for a flash. Until the lacquer dries.

Versailles

The borders of the countries on the earth's crust
hold less than the frostwork on my window. The tree
gets dressed. Breaks. You whisper and splash with ice.
I hug you and brush you. I remove your teeth,

like piano keys, then put them in again. Now you are
different: evolution has leveled the trauma.
They will bite again and flash, they'll rob you
of your sadness. I'll blow you up and pop you again

and again, don't be afraid, I won't get tired. The skin
needs care and bait. And sometimes you have twelve floors
and we have to figure out immediately if you're a match.

To cut deeper and deeper into your taste. And also: to gently
herd them back, the pedestrians who tumbled out of your wing
at the silliest hour. You are Slovene, therefore sad.

Who's Standing

Are you the stone of a fruit, dear soul? Mandorla, fetus
in white coffee? Your eyes are flames,
the dark grains of my ladies.
Shut the slot if you can't watch it.
Take a break.
My love is a holdup lifting you slowly,
slowly, so the air doesn't run out.
The tears you never confessed to fell
into soup bowls, in a Slovene
village inn. The shawl was
green, red, from Kashmir,
We lost it then.
But you are cube in me,
little light burning endlessly on the grave.

I watched the ascent, the food,
your blood pulsing on different continents.
Tunnels in parallel worlds
collapsing.
In the fire we saved
the sizzle of your tennis shoe. I pasted you up
with resin, with tokens, so you could breathe
only through your rhomboids.
I shoed you or
cleared the sky when I
starved you, when I taped up
your gargling.

How much longer will I be cut into pieces?
Loaded among wooden logs.

Earth

Koper defines darkness. Mothballs of circumcision
go to Cannes. Say you traveled under and over the earth,
returning like stitches. I didn't. The engineer

leveled my swim across his drawing board. Water!
My yellow Ami boiled over. The same with the homeopath
questioning the spawner: he can't

hope for the truth. The meetings were always
the previous ones. When they bring shrouds, compasses,
bibs – did you add something to the signature? You

don't know if moss drips from your tongue. There are
submissions. Trees tied together like braids
that rub together. A guarantee is a long hair. Small

is the body, huge the fin, and what you call
brutality: self-evident. Touch this
landscape beneath her. I don't want to watch

them torture pancakes. They're lusty. You
are all lusty. They all anoint the circle of the sun.
Virgins, foam, fish. We leap over her

along with density. Between the first and second
breaths the sex veers, it wants every fruit.
Violence tears water apart and plucks lint. The miracle

keeps occurring. When the wood pile before
the mountain cabin is torn down, and a cricket,
a fugue, and a *cantilena* are the same: utter bliss.

Riva

Fishermen's nets hang from the mouths of giants,
your eyes, flamingo, and your gray full-breasted flank.
Cranes are robbing steamers. At the top

of the gangway: "To your berths!" Cows' feet hang
like the broken teeth of a comb. Sparks erupt. Waiters
pin diamonds to the tablecloths, and at Hvar,

in front of the movie theater, someone's begging
to return the wallet I lost. Dikan got
to Vera. I took Branko's sister. Years later,

when we were smoking Kents: "When will you graduate?"
When I graduate I'll travel around the world. The blacks
hurled the junkie from the deck because he

urinated. He didn't lift the broom. You fought
with your grandfather. You couldn't
write. You survived because of the cold weather. You're used

to walking on ice. On Crete your skin blisters,
on huge gray stones still warm in December. Doctor
Jamnicki is coming back. If a hen is tied up

as a chick it will stay tied up. Nurses won't bite her.
During the night she walks with a jug on her
head, on the parquet floor. No paintings in our house.

The walls are round. Your hair is horsehair. *Che xe*
viniù da vicin, anche te ga crollà tutta tua roba sporca. Mi?
Chi te ga crollà? And the anxiety of lifting the lid

of the piano, the flash of the eyes. The procession
at the feast of Corpus Christi, huge bicycles
on the rafts. Jeti rides logs in the chute. Ashbery

at Cooper Union, 1986: "And if you did/good that's
fine, but if you did bad it don't make no
difference, you're equal/same as the others,

and the devil don't give a shit who you are or
whether your name has an umlaut to it." *Flowchart*,
Carcanet, pg. 100. That's why you can't manage *cavallotti*.

And spitting and joking, *no te capici chi voga*.
Pretty, but she doesn't dress well. Little balls,
seething beads, they swallow them for the little one.

Mákar, Kaić, *tu Dio che sii Stabile. Meglio un succo di*
pompelmo. And then again Hermes in Olympia, stolen
pajamas on the boat in Pirius. Throw yourself on the needles.

Isolani, pescecani. No way. No way at all, not
even if you want to. Who will get the milk? You've already got
the lederhosen. *Ma Dio, chi xe viniù sta sera. Dai,*

dai, butta xo ciapin. Did Hera avenge him
with fried polenta? Mozart wasn't shy,
he didn't stop staring. We kill English

kings. We're feeding the cartridge clips. Lynda's father
laundered money for the Mafia. She's walking with her pillow,
writing *Ghost Money*. The humble one, the silent

chicken is swallowing cubic meters of the sublime.
The thing is, parents have to limp. Or tell them
you were crawling over emptiness. Over everything white.

Everything in drizzle. Everything in the snowbound forest
tied to the Mediterranean. At the second lake, yes, I heard,
at the composers' hut – last year he was bitten

by the tsetse fly, he didn't come back from Africa.
The same one who said you have to splatter
your ego everywhere. I forget his name. I have

little crocodiles on my tongue, without a story.
Beetles are nibs. The secret addition
to human hair. You see, if death catches me, the white

mass will stay, pudding we'll fight over. Supply
is not the problem. What is it then? Flickering
lights in Janitio, an Oriental regard? Railroad tracks

crushed, arms ripped out. In the Venetian mirrors
they licked the connections. *No te xe vecio, te ghe diría,*
si, che te diría. Mai da un lado. The atmosphere

brought back the Breceljs and Beblers. The Bogomils
vanished and married. This is our jamboree. And
we won't dig up any flowers, they're protected.

Translated from Slovene by Christopher Merrill and the author

A Conversation with Tomaž Šalamun

Editor Jeffrey Young met with Tomaž Šalamun at his home in Ljubljana during the first week of August. They recorded a conversation, of which the following is an excerpt.

Šalamun: It is the opening of language which starts. The first step can be just surrender. It can be a happy surrender, and through this, it's like an animal would come out. A beautiful dove would come out through this surrender, which is language, and you follow. When the language is really going, is really making itself, there can be no doubt. If I would allow doubt at that moment, I would be like a runner who is thinking of his legs. I don't have time to doubt, I have to be absolutely there, not to lose a microsecond or to allow a microspace to come in between what happens, because this could block the whole process. Sometimes I have the feeling that I'm just getting up and stepping directly into some place, and I experience it as someone would whip me, or that flowers would cover my head or my face. And this would be language. Language is the material or the substance that comes from this meeting, this coming together. When it happens it's a miracle, a jump, a delight. Sometimes I feel that I am screaming from delight, but also from awe. I give whatever I have to it.

Young: Is this an inner world that you're describing?

Šalamun: It's a presence, a clarity. I don't see if this is outside of me or inside of me. I see it in the space where I am, or in the space toward which I am going, because I am seeing. It may not be palpable in terms that I would touch it, or even understand it, but I perceive it, I describe it, so it's real, otherwise I wouldn't be able to write it. If this were invention, it wouldn't be sustainable as language. There are many times when one wants to get the heat for writing, and then you do write, but you have to stop because there is no life in it. It's not real. It didn't really happen. You only wanted it to happen. And these are big sins. This can be really damaging for the process, because it means that you were in hubris. I think that language melts the self, the self is just gently overpowered and becomes part of heaven, part of a void, which is at the same time the utmost of fullness, transparency, and translucence. But writing can also be diabolical, because it cuts things apart, it goes very deep and makes space and touches places we probably should not touch. But the diabolic position does not come from dark, it comes from light, from wanting to bring light as far as it can go. Sometimes the language is very happy and it does things like a dolphin, it is pure grace, you just follow grace, and you have this feeling of water and light. The dolphin is the language. You don't know what it is. It's important that you don't lose faith in going toward it. I have enough faith to just jump, to be a part of it, to go with it. I describe what I see. It's like the inside of an atom or the inside of a giant. I can start to describe those giants, those creatures who are probably guards and watchmen who are there to scare us. But if you know the process, you don't get scared. If you are initiated enough you know that they are watchdogs for people who are less initiated. You know that they cannot damage you.

Young: And poetry itself is a process that initiates you?

Šalamun: Poetry is a parallel process to spiritual development. As in religion, you are trained how not to be scared. As in the cabala or in dervish dances, you are trained how to be with the world as long as you can endure it. Language takes you forward, and you endure as long as you can endure. But still, there is this constant fear of being too diabolic, that you will be punished for what you are doing, because when you write you compare with God, you are doing as much as you can to the utmost borders, to the deepest wounds, as much as you can sustain, and if in the procedure something goes wrong, you can go crazy, you can become impure, you can get sick. Language can drive you toward madness or suicide as the wounds in love can drive you toward the longing to disappear. I'm not afraid that I would commit suicide, but there were several times in my life that I was afraid that suicide would come onto me as an external force that would just crush me. When it went toward me once, I experienced it as the end of the world, an earthquake. I just jumped out of the car and lay down in a field and waited like a deeply wounded animal. I had the experience that suicide would come onto me as completely dark, this utter destruction, total cold, total darkness, total nothingness. This is very complicated. It is a mixture of grace, a mixture of punishment, of enjoyment, in a way it is resignation. Resignation is when you lose faith, when you don't want to fight for it, when you are so wounded you don't believe in what you wanted before, when you punish yourself, when you feel guilty about some possible mistakes in the process, how you fought for it but didn't get it and you put down your goals and say, I give up. Resignation comes from the split between where you would like to be and where you are now and that you've lost the faith to have it again, to be there again.

Young: What is it that you have faith in?

Šalamun: Maybe I will start with joy. Just sticking with joy, maybe this is faith. If I lose faith then I don't write. I just wait. I'm defeated. I don't have energy. Poetry has to be completely open, it has to be there, it has to discover spaces which were not discovered, it has to be very courageous. Of course it can come to points which are dead or destructive. It happened to me. I came to borders which were absolutely dark, absolutely cold. It was as if everything was taken out of me. The gift for language was just taken away. I was punished. I was completely tormented. It took a certain period of time before I could calm down and for the guilt to go away, because when you make a mistake you know it through the feeling of guilt, that you have transgressed in such a way that everything can be taken out of you, or that you can be destroyed, even physically. I would have a very hard time explaining this, I just sense that poetic language is at the same place as physics after nuclear weapons, that it is more dangerous than it was before. Definitely the punishments can be as strong as in terrible weapons. It is therefore important not to sell out and to develop intuition and a sense of not falling off the gentle pattern of the world. One has to be aware of not being manipulative. Poetry has to have ground, has to fight mirrors, has to fight media, has to not give away what was always there to protect humans. It's harder and harder to break through these mirrors, these glasses, to not be caught in these incredibly complicated angles and different spaces. Mirrors are dangerous, mirrors are a trap. Mirrors end something, because they destroy nature, they forget about organicity, they are completely liquid, they are completely free, they are completely manipulative. For example, if the war is going on, and the pain is real, and you make it all too visual and repeat it for so long that the link between pain and what you see is destroyed – this is very dangerous, this is when we humans are part of it, and we have to fight against it. Language is a tissue which connects these things so that they cannot come completely apart. To develop language, to make it strong and fresh, you have to constantly travel to the spaces across the line and bring it back. Language has to go to these places to be powerful enough to protect us. But both the language of power and poetic language are hidden. They travel through initiation, and they have to stay hidden. They cannot open up or be enlightened completely, otherwise the structure of the world, the bones of the world, would fall apart. This is what happens in revolution, that one group just enters the secrecy of the initiation of power and takes it out. This ends in blood, always. The poet's role is not to allow slaughter and blood. And it's like language gets its food in the most dangerous areas, and you have to bring it back safely. States of awkwardness come out of mistakes, come because of sins, because of what is put in between, because of what is damaged. Evil is sins and mistakes, dead parts, dead times. In this way I'm Gnostic, I'm not Christian. I don't know very much about hell. Dante described it so completely that I'm not interested in it. Suffering is sins and mistakes. Evil is not there. It's just a moment on the way.

Aamer
HUSSEIN

This Other Salt

I'm running through the long grass down a slope that leads to the sea. The sun's about to set. A causeway of gold-edged steely light stretches across the darkening water, from sky to reddish sand. It's a holiday. I'm at the beach with my parents, ready to leave for the islands. Minutes before the boat sails, my mother tells my father to let me have some money for the apples I want to buy. She's dressed in green; my little sister in her light blue sunsuit clings to her hand. My father wears eggshell summer linen.

I'm ten.

I make my way to where the hawkers sit with piles of nuts, candy, plastic dolls. But I ignore their calls: I know what I'm looking for. The man with the parrot, who tells long stories and sells red apples.

– How much, I ask as I point to a big red apple.

– Two rupees. He holds up two fingers.

– You're joking. It's wormy. I'll give you eight annas.

He makes the V sign again.

– I'll pay you two rupees for your parrot.

– My parrot's a treasure. He tells stories about kings.

– He's made of cloth. He's got worms. He eats worms. You can feed him your apples. So there.

– But you can have this for free, he says, holding up a great green ripe pear.

When I wake up, I'm thinking of Lamia. Lamia, who left Palestine when she was seven, and at thirty-four Beirut, where she had come of age and painted some of her most beautiful pictures. Exile after exile after exile: Egypt, Lebanon, Paris, London, New York, and finally Indonesia. First with her Reuters-reporter husband, then, more often, alone in pursuit of new visions. After the civil war she wouldn't paint faces; she said their callousness made her retch. She painted in oils, seascapes and golden fruit, sculpted in stone, metal, or clay, and then painted her pieces in gold or other colors. She made me a golden pear for my thirtieth birthday, soon after I had the first of the recurring dreams. Golden Lamia, usually so optimistic, got very drunk with me one afternoon many years ago, when I'd told her I had to leave her, to look for what I'd lost in other places. She said:

– My paintings are shit. Lies and shit. There's no escape. I'll tell you the truth. That's all we have, you know.

– What, Lamia?

– Pain. It keeps us together. Not you, not me, I mean. Everyone. We're born in it and to it. Even when you think it's love, it's pain – it draws you together, makes you imagine you're two, separates you, tears you apart – you think it's love, but it's always pain, Sameer, only pain.

Then we began to make love on the carpet, but naked and joined to me she winced and flinched, pushed me out of her, pushed me away, and said:

– It hurts too much.

I took it for a physical reaction. I looked at her, naked with her small breasts and her wide hips, her thick wild hair knotted up because of the heat, and thought how I'd told her once: When you're dressed you look like an empress, when you're naked you're a goddess. I used to hang grapes in her hair. Afterward we faked sleep in each other's arms. Now I'm not so sure what was hurting her, the coming together or the breaking apart, the fact or the metaphor. Probably both.

Nearly January: the last Saturday of another futile year. The winter hasn't chilled; it's what I call mushroom weather, like humid soup or mutton stew gone cold. It's been raining, in that distressed London way that keeps you locked indoors watching junk TV, trying to read or work or think, smoking twenty cigarettes a day and downing half as many instant coffees, remembering other seasons, other spaces, too lazy or too tired to try leaving town. I decided not to go East this winter; told myself I couldn't afford it, that annual return as a privileged tourist playacting a homecoming, that vicarious living of other people's lives. I'd do some writing instead. I suppose another reason for my hanging on is Tara. But I spend far too much time waiting for her, talking on the telephone, observing other people's pain, too lazy to live my own, too exhausted to search for it. I've finally found a temporary home; I live in a state of longing, all year round.

The coming of April will turn me forty. My slim volume of stories has been out a year, a minor occurrence in my life, even an anticlimax. I dedicated it to Lamia, who died very quietly nearly two years ago, in the April that followed our farewell trip. Cancer had already become her lover that Indonesian summer. I never saw her again, though she lived to see her fifties. Her voice had faded and she'd started to limp, so they tell me, and she didn't want me to see her like that, with her reddish hair sparse again after chemotherapy, she wouldn't have. But the last time I spoke to her and told her love had come to nothing and I was still on my own and proud of it, she said she really wanted to see me give myself to one person, to stop being afraid that no one had enough to give because that only masked my own dread of giving myself up. Giving doesn't mean surrender, she said. Give someone a chance, and settle. Before I leave you forever, she meant. Michel, her journalist husband, with whom she'd argued so violently about politics and everything else, went back to her and nursed her in those last months. She died in Jakarta, a city she loathed. I think she wanted her body to be burned in Ubud, but in her last moments she decided that serene Javanese faith gave her peace, and she lies in a Muslim cemetery she chose in Yogyakarta. Later, when he could travel to Palestine, Michel wished he had encouraged her to decide on cremation; he'd have taken some of her ashes to Beirut and their youth and the rest back to Jerusalem to rest in the soil that gave birth to her. She went quietly, he told me over wine when I traveled to France to collect the paintings she'd left me. Quietly as she'd lived, I replied. I'm the only one who could tell them that they'd always imagined her footsteps, which didn't exist; she never made a sound.

And Hobnail, the erratic and inspired Anglo-Australian who spent the days of a summer season showing Lamia the distant secret places of Southeast Asia to subsidize his sex tourism and its nights hunting and buying young Asian flesh – Hobnail's dead too. How strange a pair they'd made, the frail gray-eyed auburn-haired woman dressed as a haute couture gypsy, graceful even in her fading, and the skinny bald man whose tight holiday denim didn't hide his growing pot, the two of them wandering around the sacred spots and ruins of Bali and Java.

In every city, Hobnail would find a lover, and that summer I was there with Lamia and he latched on to us, we were burdened with his findings. Dinner here, dinner there, and he never had enough to pay; we were left to pick up the charges for him and for his companion of the moment. From time to time, when he was bored, he'd try to force his stories on me or ask to share my room to save himself some money. His name was Hobbs; I called him Hobnail because he always intruded, heavy-booted, on my privacy. Lamia had called him Hannibal in a delicious Arab accent, with the emphasis and a guttural semi-vowel on the second syllable. Later, we had no other name for him but Hobnail.

But there's one scene that stays with me. We're on our way out of Jakarta. The companion of the moment arrives, Andy from Medan. Hobbs leaves us, spends some time with him until the announcer barks: Time to board for Denpasar. Michel runs toward them. There's a moment that looks like an altercation, then money changes hands between Michel and Andy, the customary payoff. Hobbs joins them, comes back, and then I understand him, though it'll take me months to realize it. It's his face I recognize, riven with pain, suddenly old – the ugly face of love.

His death did make a sound. OUR MAN IN SOUTHEAST ASIA BATTERED TO DEATH BY REFUGEE RENT BOY. Scandals boiled in the tabloids. He'd come back to London to write a book about Indonesia. He was seeing Alex, an Eastern European man aged about twenty, someone he'd met outside a pub and taken up with. Alex had asked for a light or a cigarette and Hobbs had realized that what he really wanted was a meal. He was starving, he smelled of poverty. Alex had assumed he was to reward the meal with little sexual favors. It wasn't really sex at all, Hobbs was to say, more a question of company and pity. But the pity dried up when Hobnail found out the guy was seriously on the game. Hanging around pubs and street corners, turning tricks for twenty quid a time, Alex had been picked up by someone in Oxford Street who turned out to be a plainclothesman, and when he got caught they of course found out that he was cheating on his dole and his application for refugee status was provisional. Alex passes on Hobnail's name as a contact. No good for a leading foreign correspondent still remembered for his youthful exposés of the Sukarno days. Hobnail refuses to acknowledge him. He doesn't want to know.

So when Hobnail gets done on the way to his flat – battered to death, actually, with a trashcan lid, near Marchmont Street – it's the Bosnian who takes the blame. Actually, Alex was a Romanian, but he lived the way people here expect Bosnians to live, or Algerians, so the tabloids left out the Bucharest bit.

Somehow, I don't believe Alex killed Hobbs, though his defense wasn't very convincing. He looked too hapless – in contrast to Hobnail's sharp-toothed Balinese boys – that time Hobbs had turned up with him at a book signing I did. I'd had to talk to them, though I didn't want to; I remember the boy had bad teeth, two or three of them were blackened or gold, and I wondered why Hobbs hadn't forced him to have a bath before bringing him out in public. Alex. I remembered his name for the way Hobbs had said it, in that manner he had which announced someone permanently, helplessly enthralled by love. Perhaps Hobbs had reprimanded Alex, played the putative father, said the unsayable. Perhaps there'd been an accident.

I wonder who Hobbs loved when he died; or if it was that hunger, the endless hunger I'd seen in his eyes the morning at the airport, that led him to take home with him someone who was strong enough to brandish iron. Because that's how it went, the reported story. People had seen him walk down from Russell Square to his apartment block with a small young man. They hadn't seen his companion's features, because he had on a jacket with a hood, like Alex's jacket of cheap pink imitation silk.

Colors looked different to Lamia in the last months of her life: she was always in search of reds, and fire entranced her. Indonesia had made her paint faces and figures again. She did a series of nude bathers on the banks of the Agong River. She always thought the miniatures were incomplete. I wonder what Michel has done with them. He couldn't understand her work, couldn't keep up with her changing vision.

I suppose it was in search of fire that Hobnail took us to a royal cremation in Gyanyar. The funeral pyre was high; the ceremonies lasted till nightfall, with fires blazing all around us. Families had exhumed their hastily buried dead, to consign them to the flames on this omened day. The hawkers were out in hordes, peddling nuts, handicrafts, fried food rolled up in banana leaves; beers changed price as you bargained. A little boy adopted me: he played with my shoes and sat quietly in front of me for a long time. He got up only once, to urinate. He refused food; finally, he accepted a rambutan from my shoulder bag, and turned his back to me to eat it. Lamia sketched in a trance. I was trying to avoid the scent of death; in pagan Bali, it mingles with the perfume of cempaka and cloves. I could see death in Lamia's eyes. I didn't want to know. I wrote a postcard to Tara, wanting her to see Bali as I saw it. I bought the Ramayana sketched on a palm-leaf scroll for her that day, from a woman who tried to speak to me in Sanskrit. By sunset Lamia was exhausted. We couldn't see Hobnail anywhere. Lamia suddenly became restless; she was hot and wanted a long shower. Then I found Hobbs under a wall, rapturous in attempted intimacies with a giggling Wisnu Darmawan. Wisnu was the tall young assistant manager at our Ubud hotel, requisitioned by Hobbs to be our guide in Bali though he was as lost in Gyanyar as we were.

In spite of being named after the Hindu god who reincarnated as the Balinese hero Rama, Wisnu was a Javanese migrant and, as it turns out, the son of pious Muslims. He'd been on the island about a year. His only contribution to our excursion was to take turns with Hobbs at the wheel of the kijang, and every time we stopped for a drink or a walk he'd look for creepers bearing flowers that shrank when they were touched. He called them shy princesses. Once Hobbs made the unforgivable mistake of asking where the best roast pig in Bali was to be found. Wisnu paled.

– Too many porks in Bali everywhere, he muttered. Balinese people keeping too many porks. We don't keep porks in Jogja. Only Chinese people growing porks in Java.

We realized he liked Lamia and me because he thought of us as people of the Quran. Lamia told me she found him so exquisite she wanted to paint him as a half-naked Solonese court dancer. She had her way: he appeared in a sarong one evening at the Agong. He'd probably put away his scruples about the shameless infidel Balinese because of the heat. She did a beautiful gouache impression of him in movement, gold and ochre and white; the hands and eyes and the tilt of the head were all his. Later, when I saw the Ramayana performed in the kraton of Yogyakarta, I could see: the dancer who played Rama, in his height and limbs and smile, could have been Wisnu Darmawan's twin. Maybe Lamia had seen Wisnu through Hobnail's eyes. It was Hobbs who looked up at Wisnu as though he were a god.

While Lamia slept, I'd sit on the terrace, smoke my clove-rich kreteks and draft my story – or think about it. It was inspired by something that had happened to me in Leyden, the year before. I had left Suhayla, my on-again, off-again lover of the time, in London. Lamia and I were spending a few days in a flat that had been lent to us by a friend. Below our windows, the swan-speckled river sluggishly ran. It was Easter. We'd been told that someone had committed suicide there not long before. The first night we were there, we couldn't sleep; the wind blew savage outside and the rain screamed. Lights switched themselves on and off and the bathroom was so cold it was impossible to go in. Lamia, usually intrepid, was trying to remember the prayers of protection she'd long since rejected. The next night was rainier and the atmosphere even more tumultuous. A terrible banging came from the direction of the front door, but there was nothing there I could see. I finally went into the bathroom; a window hung loose on its hinge as if a night thief had just escaped. A cloud of clove-scented smoke hung in the air. In the morning, our host – a Dutch woman married to a Sumatran poet – came back from Rotterdam. She told us that the tenant before had been an Indo called Mellema, who'd slashed his wrists in the bath. They'd called in an exorcist, but the restless spirit remained restless. We moved to a hotel that evening.

Being in Ubud brought back the story to me; every night there, I'd find on my bed a straw puppet of Sri Dewi, the local rice goddess, its head on my pillow. Somehow the faint repulsion the idol evoked in me brought back the Leyden incident and those horrible huge dolls young men in Italian towns buy for their girlfriends at Christmas. I thought how effective it would be to write a story with other stories concealed in it, a ghost story. A couple on the verge of parting arrive at a Balinese chalet where an Indo with the personality of Hobnail had killed himself the year before, driven mad with love for a native called Putu or

Ketut or Wayan who would have the features of Wisnu Darmawan.

Hobbs, too, had an eerie story about Bali. His own wife, a promising anthropologist, had died there, by her own hand or so it seemed, in the late sixties. Too much death and sorcery here, Hobbs would ominously say, hinting at deviltry and murder. I couldn't help thinking that Elisa Kendall-Hobbs must have caught her young husband with a Balinese lover. I'd bring all that in, a flashback. The tale within the tale would be narrated by the Balinese. The wife – I'd make her look like Tara.

The vagaries of Garuda's booking system meant that Lamia left for Yogya one night before I did. I sat on the terrace by the pool drinking iced arak and brem. When Hobnail came to join me, beer in hand, I was honest: I'm trying to write. Late that night as I sat on the terrace with a bottle of Perrier and my kretek, trying to transform Hobnail into a suicidal Indo besotted by a native he thinks is possessed by his wife, someone knocked on the chalet door. I wrapped my robe around my half-naked body, impatient; I thought the importunate Hobnail was lonely, and drunk enough to risk rebuff. I don't think he'd gotten very far with Wisnu, who probably accepted his few cheap favors with a smile and customary Javanese grace. Invaded by my characters, I thought, and I wasn't wrong. I opened the door to a laughing, bowing Wisnu, a Balinese jacket and sarong incongruous on his tall frame. He had a frangipani behind one ear.

– I didn't ask for anything.

– Champagne. He smiled.

– I think you have the wrong chalet, I said. Mr. Hobbs is two doors down.

– Compliments of the management, he said, and pushed past me with champagne and seasonal fruits on a tray he set down on the table: mangos and mangosteens, miniature bananas, rambutan, grapes, pears, and a pineapple.

It was my last night on the island. He was already opening the bottle: I felt I should offer him some of the champagne. He wasn't a waiter, and he'd been willing to help us all through our stay. He accepted the glass silently. He talked all night. He had a wife and a son in Yogya. He was going back, taking the plane tomorrow, to be there during the Mouloud festivities for the Prophet's birthday.

He should have left for town hours ago; that's where he had been living. I told him he could go down to Denpasar with me if he liked, in Hobnail's jeep, hired at Lamia's expense. He should wait at the gate. We rested a little, I on the bed where Lamia had lain only hours before, he on mine. He left as dawn broke, barefoot through the French window over the damp grass among the overhanging banana leaves. I sluiced myself with water from a barrel in the outdoor sunken bath, naked under the open sky, leaves squelching beneath my feet. I watched a tiny olive lizard I'd dislodged run up a betel palm.

On the way to the airport, Hobnail's eyes and smiles had little chains of knives in them.

– What was he like? he asked me at the airport. Wisnu had discreetly removed himself, to buy us cold beers, I think.

– Who?

– Don't act the innocent, Sameer. Was he good? I saw Wisnu leave your room this morning.

– Not bad, I sneered. Not bad at all.

In Yogyakarta, Wisnu got in touch and drove Lamia and me out to Solo and Candi Sukuh, and showed us some of the most beautiful little mosques in town, which Lamia loved because men and women prayed there side by side; the act of prayer was a simple part of living. He took me to the finest food stalls. I remember the nasi gudeg we ate with our fingers the night I left, rice lush with spices and jackfruit. He still writes, but for awhile I haven't replied.

I never wrote the Balinese ghost story I'd planned. Hobbs couldn't make the transition into a haunted Eurasian; death and realities got in the way. Handsome Wisnu and Ubud aren't in my book. I finished it instead with fictions carved out of my own life. I wrote about the fallen smell of fruit: gold papaya flesh spilling over marbled green skin onto white stone, ants ravishing its fallen sweetness. About the fallen smell of rain, the vapor rising off my skin as I stood in the melon patch burning with the freshness of the shower. About the fallen music of the past, its shattered notes calling out the night's name, the name of someone I had lost which once was Layla, like a woman singing or the sea breaking into white foam on white rocks, like the rain on a May night. I wrote about the city by the sea, hers and mine, of home as a forgotten song, a shared language, common consummation like bread. I wrote about my longing for another tongue, a mother tongue, the language of my longings, liquid, whispering, sibilant. I suppose by the time I reached its end I knew the call of home was gone, I had written about a Karachi that was lost, that I had left twenty-five years ago, and then I was looking for light again. But my book ended with images of all my cities on fire. Karachi had been in flames for years; I knew I couldn't keep on grieving for that contagion. Then Bombay, too, that other city by the sea that had served for years as a surrogate home, was in mourning for the riots that had ravaged it a year to the day before the last time I was there, a year ago. I'd thought of going on to Pakistan, but at the airport I changed my ticket and stopped for a night at an unfamiliar city in the Gulf. There I could see the sea and the sand of remembered places.

When I came back, my mirrors of belonging had cracked, because I hadn't been able to see my face in them, and in London, too, the cracks in the painted glass were widening. Lamia had been dead almost a year. I tried to reach out to Tara, even to lean on her, though I'd been trying to renounce all hope of winning her, but she couldn't carry my widening despair for more than a day. Tara, though she wasn't even born there, kept returning to Karachi every year, bringing back reports of a city that wasn't mine, that I have to let go of.

Tara was putting down deeper roots in London, locating herself in a rhetorical space of blackness that had little resonance for me, falling in love with an ugly wild-haired bisexually charismatic performance poet – more of a stand-up comic, really, who celebrated ethnic music and cooking. Kim also told jokes about S&M and dykes and leather that I couldn't pretend to understand; she wrote politically incorrect ditties about hybrids, which because she was mixed race herself made me laugh unwillingly when Tara dragged me – or I dragged myself behind her – to a joint in the East End to see her perform.

So now I'm trying to work on something else, something that holds off thoughts of Hobbs and his life and death, something kinder, a story that keeps me in the light, or perhaps the light on me: a critical biography of an intriguing couple from Lahore, writers at the turn of the century who ran their own press and published their own novels and stories. An idealized life, almost a myth, into which I could imagine myself and Tara. With a suitably tragic end that I could have done without, though; the wife died at the age of thirty. Tara turned twenty-seven last June. And she's changed from the Tara of two years ago, with her scholastic inclinations and her preoccupation with political movements and social causes. Tara who wanted to go home and crusade for women's rights, minority rights, the rights of the poor. She tried out Islamabad; she lasted a month. But right now it's love and money she cares about. She works for a leading production company, uses her academic credentials. Tara will live forever. It's Lamia who died young. Michel told me that Wisnu was one of her pallbearers. His family keeps an eye on her grave.

There's another part to my dream, too. Post-intermission. When I look at the shore, I see my parents, wildly waving.

– Come on now, you'll miss the boat, they seem to say.

As I run down the slope to the sea, I trip on a rock, lose a slipper. If I run on, my mother will scold me for losing my sandal; if I stop to look for it, I'll miss the boat. Trouble either way. Finding it, at least, will show her I'm responsible, a man. But that can come later. The sky's nearly dark, but I'm not afraid of the falling night. I want my pear. I dig my teeth into its tart freshness. I look at the boats, which wave their bright banners on their way to distant islands. When I finish my fruit, I'll dig my fingers and toes into the taut moist sand, I'll build a fortress, I'll write my name or a story.

I've never really understood this part of the dream, and the dreamscape belongs only there. There's no long grass on Karachi's beaches. Maybe it's the shore of Beirut, or a riverbank in Bali. All I can hear is the sound of the sea of tongues: père leaves son, leaves with mère by mer: son devours pear (fruit or father) with one foot bare. One shoe of identity gone from my foot (in my mother tongue, pair). So in the end, it's a dream about parents and tongues, and about being alone, and I'm sure Lamia's there, too, because she spoke perfect French and painted fruit and spent her life between land and sea. Because remember, love always tastes like the fruit of Eden, flavored with the forbidden, threatening as incest. Dark feelings fall, even on my search for light; no Manicheanism for me, as I say to my friend Maryam who tells me of the sequence of poems about light she's writing. Sometimes it's easier to deal with death than with desertion, so my visions find their way into the true story I'm researching; icons of Lamia, lurid red posters of Tara, images of myself, finally loved, finally loving.

It's the last day of the year; one of those days when things keep inventing themselves around you so that you're always one step behind the day. You feel needed, maybe even wanted. That's usually because you've planned with such care, of course, not to stay alone. So the things you really wanted to do, the places you wanted to be in, don't remember you, and if they do, it's too late. I've revolved like a 45 rpm all day, I'm hyperventilating.

This time, though, I thought it wasn't going to be that way. Kim's been cheating on Tara for days, can't settle down, plays around, wants to fly, wants to be chained. Last week Tara chased Kim out, told her to clean up her act, get her head examined. And then she spent days in agony, cramped with menstrual or premenstrual tensions, crippled with doubt and need. My moment to step in. Only, I said to myself, because I'm lonely, and so is she; I gave up on anything other than friendships and Plato two years ago. If I have a companion now, it's Lamia – the Lamia of thirteen years ago, merged with the Lamia of Bali. I see her pale small foot, white and gold at the same time, remember looking at it and touching it, feeling then that I'd once known a love for her so unbearable that I'd had to destroy it before it destroyed me, I'd had to go away and tell her I was going, and there in our Ubud chalet I knew that it was still unbearable, that if anything, my desire for Tara made me love Lamia more, without need or anxiety. I knew, too, that the fresh desire was born of that earlier passion, younger and more raw, it was a replay and a reenactment, that if I hadn't been broken and ridden and broken again by Lamia all the way from Istanbul to Christmas I'd never have imagined loving Tara at all. I kissed Lamia's foot there and cried, hoping that my tears wouldn't awaken her and yet wanting her to know that I wasn't crying for her death, which I knew would come soon, but because all my love for her was in this other salt, more than it had ever been in all our nights of anguished loving, and I had to give it to her before she went, it was too heavy for me to carry, all this bitter crystal salt, without her in the world. I think she knew, because after a tactful silence she opened her eyes and asked for a pillow and a glass of water and when I brought them to her she said:

– Couldn't you just die here, with all this around you? I want to be burned here. Or buried in the mountains.

I looked through the open sliding screen doors and saw tall trees, flowers white yellow and red ensconced like candle flames high high above us in the green turquoise sky, and fiery rocks bending over them, the roaring silver Agong River below. The air was full of life: dragonflies, spiders spinning from branch to branch, black little birds. And I knew I still wanted to live, even without her, even if living set me on fire.

In Ubud the scent of cloves was overpowering. Bougainvillea bloomed in such profusion we forgot to count its colors. (Now and then we see a wild and earnest rose.) At night I sat among the mosquitoes, daring them to take me, challenging their venom with mine. Fireflies rose toward the waning moon. Soon after sunset the musicians would set up their threnodies. The flute mourned over the clinking aphonic keys of the gamelan. Earlier, in the afternoon, the same melody would play for the butterfly troupe of little girls from the ballet school; shoulders out, hands twisting, the children danced to the clapping and the *lero-lero-lero* chanted by their maestro. The fragrance of frangipani filled the air; each musician had a flower tucked behind an ear. (Between rehearsals, the children run to the ornamental pond to scoop up tadpoles and little fish in their palms. Once on the mountain path a child approaches us and points, wordless, to our basket. Lamia thinks he wants her mineral water. *Angur, angur,* he finally says: the word for grapes is the same in his tongue and mine.) And there on the mountain as the colors of the day flowed into each other, I'd think about love. Or the lack of it, the gap where need might be. I still wonder what the words of the song meant, the *lero-lero-lero* of the afternoon's chant transposed into words in the evening, possibly words of love.

(I'm walking down the hill to the Agong when I first hear the song. It's afternoon. The hill is steep and I'm drenched in sweat, slipping in my soft leather shoes. Lamia, that fish, has changed her form; she leaps down the pathway like a goat, perhaps to prove that her sickness hasn't vanquished her. At the river the naked old women soak their sagging breasts in the sun while sons brush their teeth and daughters-in-law in fancy underthings wash clothes. A young woman pulls me into the river, helping me down the stones with the strength of two men. Soon I'm in the water with the bathers. Lamia sits on a rock, talking to a sarong-soaked Wisnu. Drops and rivulets glisten on bare backs brown and black. The fierce light burns my arms an even deeper bronze. I clear the water to join Lamia. For a moment I think she's sleeping. When I'm wreathed in the clove-heavy smoke of my silent cigarette she starts talking. Then I tell her about Tara, how I met her one night at a club I'd been dragged to by friends and how since then she's never gone away. But Lamia's looking at Wisnu, who's taken my place in the water. For an instant, something shoots through me: perhaps I miss someone.)

I thought of the preparations we were making for her dying, of Lamia leaving me forever and of the pain I'd never really learned to feel, the pain of someone leaving, maybe that's what you call love. But for me, with Lamia no longer mine, absent but close, it was there and it was something else, I wouldn't call out to it or give it a name. It was something that stayed with me, it melted into the colors and the bird song and the light rain, it cried in the night and pulled me close to shadows I wouldn't see in daylight. It called when the day was ending, when the sky changed from blood orange to purple smoke, beckoned to me when the first two stars emerged, became a third star. It couldn't obscure the moon, it was the moon.

I didn't understand the kind of love that needed one person. I felt that desire grew in me, I carried it within myself. Maybe that was Lamia's gift, that desire for the sky, the colors and the changing and the light, for the pain and everything that went with it. When you're in a place so strange to you, far from everything you know, when you travel at all, you lose your skins one by one until only the seventh and innermost layer is left, you become nothing. You see your future as some kind of dream you can stage yourself. That's one of the gifts of being nothing anymore. So I went back to London longing for Tara or for my dreams of her and of what I could be for her, prepared to give her what I had, only to find that she'd already come as close to me as she ever would. But some part of her was still there, tied to me, her loneliness maybe, and the recognition of mine, or some vestige of desire.

There's a poem by Charlotte Mew copied out in Tara's hand in one of my notebooks. It's called "A Quiet House." Tara recited it to me two months after we met, the first time I told her about breaking up with Suhayla, about how destructive a relationship can be, even when you aren't in love, and how it leaves you pitted and scarred, even if just for a little while. Shell-shocked, I said I was.

Red is the strangest pain to bear,
In Spring the leaves on the budding trees;
In Summer the roses are worse than these;
More terrible than they are sweet:
A rose can stab you across the street
Deeper than any knife...

– But red doesn't hurt me at all, I told Tara when I came back from Indonesia. It makes me think of Bali and living.

Me with my memories of Lamia, Tara with the quarreling specter of Kim – two solitudes, spending the last nights of December eating nuts and chips in dismal yellow North London pubs, watching dingy comedies in local cinemas and coming out empathy-fatigued, with little left to talk about, waiting for a suitable moment to say goodbye. I've been playing the consoler and confessor, or trying to; loving vicariously, wondering whether this is better than the emptiness I've become so used to living.

Anyway, it can't be much worse. At least I'm trying to give, make myself useful, tell myself I should be unselfish. And emptiness has something in common with vicarious sexless love; there's something burning, a torch or a bush, on the other side of the white chasm in front of the confessor and the confider, something that calls you, tells you that you too will come to it in time.

I never speak to Tara about Lamia. We've planned to bring the New Year in together, quietly, at the Mata Hari – Eye of the Morning – a kitsch miniature evocation of an Orientalist's Southeast Asia. We'll eat the weirdest fruits de mer, or flambéed prawns, smoke kreteks and drink champagne. Maybe we'll even learn something new about love.

Tara's been red-hot with love all summer, all autumn – now, as the year dies, she's blue. There's that sultry saxophone whine in her voice again, phrasing endless minimalist improvisations on two notes: Love and pain, pain and love. Sometimes I think she feels she's the only one conversant with them, she's the expert but also the expert sufferer; the martyr who knows the price of joy, who knows that lovemaking is always painful, always relinquishing, an act of renunciation even when it's meant to be a taking. A little bite of death. Sometimes I agree with her, add my fewer broader notes to hers; usually I'm in counterpoint, sweeter or more salt, always patient. Sometimes I think I'll suffocate with patience. Dying's actually no problem, it's the way there that's so fucking long, so full of mirages that make me want to live again. Closer to mercy or oblivion, every winter, step by rheumatic step, I listen, I wait, I watch, I write, always talking, forever silent.

Tara's blues may be gone, though, for awhile at least. Kim's back. She swears she'll stay forever, however short that is, this time. But our night on the town's still on, à trois. So Tara tells me now. She asks on the phone just a couple of hours before we're meant to meet:

– Can Kim come with us? Otherwise she'll have to hang out with tramps in some club. She'll drive us.

Tara's voice on the wire carries in it the clash of quiet cymbals, the triumphant click of castanets. Perhaps, I think cynically, it's because I'm said to have some money in the bank;

more likely it's Tara's sense of fair play. And anticipation of the other game, less fair and more enthralling, the adventure of being with two people who love her, who will court each other to gain her favor, protect her from each other. Mistress of the night, triumphant harbinger of the coming year, she'll reign supreme.

I can't help feeling there's something predatory about Kim, something ready for the occasion, any occasion, even on a night like this, when she's working to please. Or maybe a night like this is what reveals the mercenary in her. Her eyes scan the prices on the menu; she orders a whole fish and the most expensive wine while Tara shrinks and smiles and I wave my hand in courteous dismissal. Our table, in a black glass cage, is small and fragile. Tawdry souvenirs of Java and Bali surround us, rice fields and bare-breasted Balinese on fake tapestries in faint green and coral shades, painted bright lamps, hideous leather puppets. Masks slip and are replaced. Let's go there together, we must, we have to, Kim says when Tara begins to recount my stories of Bali and Java. We dance into plans and projects: Borobudur, Prambanan, Yogyakarta, and somewhere in Sumatra, maybe Tapanuli or Lake Toba.

– Desire, Sameer, you write about desire in those stories of yours, they're your best, when you talk about love in a man's voice it could still be me, and all the women in your stories are you and still they're me. I would say it's always desire you write about.

– And what about depression? I think I write out of depression. Other peoples'. And about how they depress me too. And don't I write about death? (Hobnail's boots ride my brain again. Funeral pyres burn high in Gyanyar. In a cemetery in Yogya, Lamia's name must be written in Arabic and in Latin letters.) And love? In my next story I'm going to write about love again. It's an epic romance called "Silken Nights." Once upon a time there was a Mughal emperor who went to a New Year's feast where he fell in love with a beautiful widow who sold him a ring. For days he pined for her until the Queen his wife who loved him so much she would have sacrificed her life for him told him to take the beauteous lady to his marriage bed. But I cannot betray the lady mother of my fine sons and my pious daughters for a mere whim of lust, said the emperor. No, quoth the Queen his wife, it is, in our faith, a kind duty to protect the weak. To give the widow shelter befits your virtue and glory. So the King married the widow. But some months later the Queen, so it is whispered in the corridors of Agra fort, poisoned the lady with a garland of red red roses. And the Emperor lived happily ever after with the Queen, notwithstanding the occasional fornication, until she died and then he built the splendid Taj Mahal to shelter her mortal remains. And he wept all the remaining days of his life, with little maidens beside him to wipe his tears with their perfumed hair. The story is narrated by an immortal green parrot.

– Shut up, stop it, you lying swine, you'd never stoop so low… (Tara's choking on her drink.)

– I didn't know Sameer could be so ironical, I've never heard Sameer being so ironical. (Kim has emerged, dazed, from her unaccustomed silence.)

– *Cin cin*, I shout. Let's drink to four letter words like l-o-v-e. To pop-song cant. To that pain in the ass.

Tara's laughter, or too much smoke and sparkling grape, is making her cry. Or tears are running down her face because she thinks I'm aching for Lamia. Maybe because the color red is all she ever sees. Then I say to Kim:

– If you ever hurt Tara, I'll kill you.

But what I suppose I mean is, I'll kill you if you ever take all of her away from me. We're hamming it for all we're worth, the trusty trio. I can't deny there's something dangerous about this, dangerous because our embracing and caressing and touching and kissing in the midst of strangers saluting each other and shouting while they bury December has something erotic about it; an eroticism that's masochistic, hardly sexual at all, like public nakedness, like an unwillingly witnessed copulation. Tara's in my arms, her back against my breast, my breath grazing her left cheek, my left arm around her ribs, stroking her right side. Kim holds my right hand. I kiss the corner of Tara's mouth. Her dangling silver earring tickles my cheek. Soon her hair will make me sneeze. But she turns her head.

– Happy New Year.

I'm being kissed on the mouth by pairs of lips that have loved and kissed each other; touched by hands that pass on leftover love.

Hobnail hides in us all, I think with the irrelevant wisdom of near-drunkenness. He dies in our eyes. It's one of those rare tipsy insights that actually makes sense. It's not the buying and the selling that counts, I think, it's the desperation of holding onto someone for fear of being abandoned. It's the willingness to swallow pain within a relationship; it's the terror of living without it. Men with women or men, women with either, with or without each other in any combination, we're on a dance floor, in an arena of desire, on some enchanted island, trapped in merciless passion, rapt in slothful combat. In a dark Bloomsbury alley, on a November night, Tara holds on to Kim, stares at her like Hobbs at Wisnu or Andy. Kim hits her from behind; Tara survives, and takes her back. Hobbs' death was an accident; if Alex killed him, they were just miming the game of pain, the passion play of love.

And as for me, I've been playing Hobbs' game ever since I came back from Bali. Buy, sell, barter, exchange, it doesn't matter as long as I can keep Tara with me. And it's worn me out, worn me down. But she won't even hit me from behind; she doesn't care enough. Her occasional tendernesses are born of compassion. And boredom. Recognizing this I'm liberated, released from her. I've been clinging to ghosts, improvising love with shadows. There's no letting go I'll have to do. There's nothing to let go of. I don't have the courage to love anymore. Maybe I haven't ever loved her, only desired her desire, her love of loving, and those were never mine. Under profligate bougainvillea, on a remote shore, a lost man grieves for Lamia, who eleven years after his defection revenged herself by not dying in his arms, and for Hobbs and for Tara and even for poor wretched Alex who has the burden of a bludgeoning on his shoulders.

Leave others to grieve for their dead. Let me mourn my living, as they leave, one by one, for their islands. The songs say that only death can break some bonds, but I should have learned long ago that there are others life refuses early on to forge. Now I know that you can learn about the former kind when it's almost too late, and as for the latter, you can mistake them for the fated sort and be misled from milestone to near extermination before you know what's hit you. When I first knew Lamia was dying and began to grieve, that grief was for myself, for all those lost happenings and faces and things I hadn't admitted to. Then came the time of reckoning, the real death. As for Tara, I think our meeting was a fluke throw in a game of chance, but I've kept wanting to find out the players' names, and what they thought they'd gain. Tara said, earlier, that I want to write destiny, write my own. Maybe that's what I've been doing, living an end to my stories.

Last call at the bar. We all might live in the same state, but I'm leaving. Let Kim take care of Tara and herself. The roulette tables and the gambling dens, the winter sales, the season of tawdry bargains, all over now, time to pack up the wares, send the remainders to a thrift shop, cut your losses, pay up and leave.

– Here's a poem for the moment.

Wreathed in clove-heavy smoke, I translate Faiz:

Stay by me
My killer, my lover, stay by me
In the hour the night passes
Laughing, dancing
Jangling the violet anklets of pain.

– Don't be morbid, stop thinking about your friend.

– He wasn't my friend.

But I know she isn't talking about Hobbs. So I spend my last twenty pounds on champagne, but it's not destined, I soon find out, for the three of us or our farewell kisses. Kim wants to share it with the party. People are dancing on tables and chairs; Tara, my Balinese scarf in her hand, is doing something highstepping that looks like a flamenco, with a freckled Irishman trying to follow her twisting steps. I'm tired, I want out. Then Kim takes the revolving Tara by the arm.

– We've got to go.

– Already? (That's me, hypocritical.)

– Oh, we've got another party to go to, didn't Tara tell you? (Kim turns to Tara.) Part of the deal, huhn? I said I'd come here with you if you came with me.

Doelike, Tara's ready to leave. They ask if they should call me a cab, I should have known when they brought their car that I was to be dumped.

– We're not going your way, Sameer. (Kim.)

– Can you lend me a fiver? You said you'd loan me a tenner if I went short for the bill. I'm not walking through the bloody West End at this time. (Me to Tara.)

– I thought I'd brought more than I have. I've only got a twenty pound note left. I'll have to keep it for emergencies. There's a cashpoint at the corner, only a minute away. (Tara to me, with her love-to-help-you-but-I-can't-I-feel-so-guilty look.)

Dully sober now, I see them to their jalopy. Another kiss, another caress. I shudder at my own falseness as I touch Kim's shoulder and kiss the air beside her cheek. Then, as I march into the Piccadilly night from the bank, I get pushed down from behind by a gang of four, I think, or maybe I'm seeing double. They're muffled in black wool and leather. Mugged at knife point, smacked on the face and head, I aim a fist or a few before I go down flailing. My right arm takes my body's weight, my hand's numb, my lip sore.

I sit in a whitely lit cell, until the policemen remember I'm there. The big boys smell of beer, pig fat, and vindaloo. They won't take me home in their van, but they want me to tell them what the boys who mugged me looked like. They keep pretending to write, even when I'm hesitant or quiet.

– Black, they must have been. Or Bangladeshi.

I want to reply. But my tongue won't shape the words, my head's spinning from the fists and the fall, so I say:

– I'm sorry, there were three or four of them, boys, I don't know, about nineteen, all kinds of races, maybe a girl too, I'm wasting your time, all I wanted was some other poor bugger to be spared a few pounds and for you to take me home, I've still got my travel card, so I'd best be on my way…

On Piccadilly's pavements I sit down and bleed. I wrap my Balinese green scarf around my flayed left hand and watch the cotton's color change. Another bloody year to swallow, I think, and laugh at the metaphor. I trace with my right forefinger the pictures my seeping blood paints: Tara's mouth plum-dark with wine, Wisnu's wrists raised in the mudras of Solo, the gray-green eyes of Palestine, a sultry whining sax, leather puppets, pavilions and the Leaning Tower of London, fish, hobnail boots enchained by violet anklets, Alex's rotten teeth, funeral pyres and obituary photographs, fruit that bears the salty tang of love. In her grave, Lamia's pale foot taps in time to the gamelan. Wild and earnest roses bloom high among Ubud's green leaves. Tara, my stained scarf tied sash-fashion around her waist, a frangipani behind her ear, is dancing. Behind her flits the gaudy butterfly troupe. She tosses her fatal roses up in the air to the music of the *lero-lero-lero* and I wonder what color my scar will be.

Benny

BARABASH

My Mother's Side

All this stuff about doing the accounting in order to know exactly "where we stand" my mom got from her mother, who did the exact same thing, even during her last days when they didn't want to keep her in the regular hospital anymore because she was already terminal, which is a special word they invented to make us feel how terrible it is to be at the end of life, like the bus terminal at the end of the journey, and if you say it slowly you really get the shivers by the end of it, and on the other hand my mother wouldn't let them take her mother to a special hospital for terminal cases, because of the experience she already had with her father, who died there like a dog.

At first they argued about what arrangements to make for her, but in the end they left her at home because she couldn't come to our house because it's on the fourth floor without an elevator – my Dad wasn't too keen on having a terminal person wandering around the house either, because he was depressed enough already, but he wasn't about to make a major issue out of it, if there was no other option then okay, he'd agree – and because she herself didn't want to, and because it was out of the question for her to stay with Beatrice, Mom's middle sister, you might as well shoot her through the head, and as for staying with Monica, Mom's youngest sister, it wouldn't do, seeing that it was a one-room apartment which men moved in and out of as often as Monica changed her stockings, and Monica was a clean girl who changed her stockings a lot, so the upshot was that she stayed at home, where there was an elevator, only she didn't use it anymore, except when that guy from the B.I. Kadishai Society Burial Services came to take her away after she died, after the ambulance doctor explained to my mother that they didn't remove dead people, they only signed the death certificate, and Mom asked him so who does remove them, and he told her look it up in the Yellow Pages, and left. Mom started looking for the Yellow Pages, all the time saying to herself *qué cagada*, which is Spanish for shit or bullshit, which is what Dad says when he can't find something, and in the end she really couldn't find it and went next door for a minute to ask the neighbors for their Yellow Pages, and I took the opportunity to go back into her mother's room and take a closer look, because before, after we'd just arrived and Mom found her there and called out Mama

Mama, but her mother didn't wake up, she wouldn't let me come any closer, ordered me to go wait in the living room, and when I asked her what had happened, she didn't answer me because she was terribly distracted, she phoned *Magen David Adom* and after she put the phone down went to the fridge to prepare her mother's medicine, and suddenly she remembered and threw the bottle into the sink and put her handbag into the freezer instead, and later on when she looked for it to pay B.I. Kadishai, I remembered where she'd put it and I showed them.

When I went back into the room she looked as if she was simply sleeping, and when I moved a bit closer I noticed a very long column of ants coming out of a crack between two floor tiles, advancing along the wall to the TV table, where they turned in the direction of the leg of the bed and climbed up it, and when they reached the blanket I couldn't see them anymore because they were the same color as the blanket, which was an excellent example of camouflage, and then all at once they came out on the white sheet, overcame the obstacle of Mom's mother's hand, disappeared into the dark hair of her wig, which she must have forgotten to take off and which was spread out on the pillow, reappeared on her pale cheek and from there entered her mouth and vanished, and when I tried to look into her mouth I couldn't see a thing, and I was sorry that I didn't always have a flashlight on me along with my tape recorder, and then suddenly I heard my mother yelling at me from behind, what was I doing in the room, and I turned and said to her your mother's got ants in her mouth, and the Yellow Pages fell out of her hands, and she looked as if she was going to faint, but she didn't faint, she ran into the kitchen and came back with a towel and ordered me to leave the room and pounced on the ants with the towel, hitting out in all directions until finally she got to her mother's mouth and there began to clean up gently.

In the meantime my Dad arrived, and Monica, and also Amalia, my mom's friend, and there was an argument about where to look in the Yellow Pages, because there was no listing under Dead or Deceased or Transportation or Removal Services, until Dad at last found Burial Societies, and the notice that jumped out at him was the one that said "B.I. Kadishai Society Burial Services," and he read it out quickly: "Let us take care of everything for you: notification of death, burial license, transportation of the deceased, funeral arrangements, notices in the press and on the street, bus rental, flowers. A mobile phone is connected to this number after working hours, wait and you will receive a reply, at your service 24 hours a day," and they really did answer right away, but they didn't arrive until four hours later, and then only one man came instead of two, his partner had a Brith just then so he had to ask my Dad to help him with the deceased, which is what he called Mom's mother, and Dad agreed. They wrapped Mom's mother up in the sheets she was lying on and put her on the stretcher and managed somehow to get her out of the bedroom, but they got stuck in the corner of the hallway and the living room, and there was a little argument between Dad and the man. Dad told him to lower his end, and the man said no, you lower your end, I know what I'm talking about, and Mom kept saying all the time I can't look, but went on looking, and then she suddenly discovered that what was keeping the stretcher stuck was her mother's hand, which had come out of the sheets and gotten wedged against the doorpost, and she screamed her hand her hand, and the man arranged her hand and said to her lady you'd better wait on the balcony with the others, meaning Monica and Amalia who were already there, and Mom said alright, but just went on looking at the stretcher.

Finally they got out of the apartment, but they had a problem with the elevator, because the stretcher wouldn't fit inside, and when they tried to hold it at an angle, Mom's mother almost slid off, and the man from B.I. Kadishai said to Dad watch out, the deceased's going to slip off at your end, and then Dad suggested that they go down the stairs, but at the bend in the stairs he said again watch out with the deceased, and in the end she really did fall, but not from Dad's end, from the man's end, and Mom said that her mother had hit her head on the stairs, and the man from B.I. Kadishai said never mind, she doesn't feel anything anymore, and Mom said that she couldn't take any more and she was going to wait upstairs, and the man from B.I. Kadishai started thinking, and in the end he told Dad to wait a minute, he would pop outside to the van and fetch a body bag for the deceased, and he went, and Dad stayed behind to watch over Mom's mother, who was lying on the floor in the way of the elevator door so that the people in the elevator who wanted to get out couldn't open the door, Dad told them to got up to the next floor, and a man inside the elevator said I've got a pregnant woman here, and Dad said it wouldn't do her any harm to walk down one flight of stairs, so they went up to the next floor and came down the stairs and asked Dad if he didn't have a more suitable place to put his parcel, and Dad said yes he did, and they asked so why put it here, and Dad replied because your apartment's locked, and the man asked if it was a parcel for them, and just then he noticed Mom's mother's hand which was sticking out of the sheets again, and he immediately grabbed hold of his wife's hand and warned her not to look because it would harm the baby, but she did look, as if she was hypnotized, and then he pulled her away and they escaped into their apartment and in the meantime the man from B.I. Kadishai came back with a black plastic bag like a garbage bag, and he and Dad put the deceased into the bag and closed the top with a special rubber band and hoisted her onto the man's back, and he bounced her around a little until he was comfortable, and then he said she's light, must have been cancer, and in this way he managed to get into the elevator, and that was the last time I saw Mom's mother, because at the funeral she was already all wrapped up.

Before Mom's mother died she had to be looked after at home, and my Mom and her two sisters, Monica and Beatrice, shared her between them, Monica on Sundays and Wednesdays, Beatrice on Tuesdays and Thursdays, Mom on Mondays and Fridays, and each of them every third Saturday, and when Mom went there she sometimes agreed to take me with her on the condition that I didn't bother her with questions, although she did let me bring my tape recorder.

It wasn't the same when we came on Mondays or Fridays. Because on Mondays we would arrive after Monica, Mom's little sister, who looked after their mother nicely, and on Fridays we came after Beatrice, the middle one – everybody knows that middle ones always have a lot of problems, but Beatrice, even compared to other middle sisters, was a different opera, as Mom says, she has no responsibility and she's not right in the head, even when she was a child they put her in a mental hospital for four months, and to this day she hasn't gotten over it, she still hasn't forgiven her mother for the electric shocks they gave her there, which I know from one of the times when she started yelling at my mom when their father was still alive.

"Don't you talk to me about helping Papa! You have any idea what electric shock is like?"

She asked my mother twice, because the first time my mother didn't answer her. And when Mom lowered her eyes and answered quietly after the second time that no, she didn't – everyone immediately feels guilty because they didn't get shocks so they don't have the right to talk about it – Beatrice said she could demonstrate on one of her children, because she hadn't been much older than Shauli "when you went and did it to me." And Mom said Beatrice I didn't do anything to you, I was already at the University then, and your condition was... And here Beatrice burst out again that they should all shut up about her condition, because there was nothing wrong with her condition, not now and not then either, and Mom said carefully okay there was nothing wrong with your condition, and Beatrice felt that Mom was admitting at long last that she was right, and she said there you are, you admit it, so what reason did you have to put me in that hell? Mom doesn't answer because she's already sick and tired of this argument, which always comes up, but in the end, after Beatrice says again and again for what reason and by what right and why, Mom tries one more time, saying she was already at the University then, and Beatrice starts smiling her scary smile and lowers her head a little and looks up at Mom from under her eyebrows and her fringe and says to her, "Who are you trying to fool? I know exactly how you influenced them against me," and nothing helps Mom, and in fact nothing helps anybody when Beatrice starts having one of her attacks, all you can do is treat her tactfully and put on an act as if everything's alright and prevent yourself from telling her what people think of her and hope that she'll drop dead or at least go away because she's capable of sticking around till morning talking without making sense, or saying the same thing over and over with little changes, like: What does he think, that if his wife's a whore I'm a whore too? No. I'm not a whore even if his wife's a whore, and even if he thinks I'm a whore, I'm not, and I'm not his wife, and his wife isn't me, whether she's a whore or not. And most of her other stories aren't suitable for children either, like her incidents in pubs, how she picked up somebody who looked like a good fuck but when she took him home he got mad at her as if it was her fault that he was impotent, which means weak, and he beat her up and forced her to suck him, and so she bit him and they had to take him to the hospital to stitch him up, they even wrote about it in the newspaper, how the doctors at Ichilov succeeded through a rare operation in saving the sexual organ of a man injured by biting during sexual intercourse, and I cut out the story and attached it to the cassette *My Mother's Sisters*, and Mom went to get Beatrice out of jail together with Amalia who brought her homo lawyer along, and all Beatrice said to the judge when he asked her why she did it was to show them they better not screw around with me, she burst out laughing and said it again, to show them they can't screw around with me, and she laughed again, so they sent her to the hospital again, and when she got out of the hospital she was very very quiet for a long time, her eyes were sad and her pretty face was swollen with yellow patches and she tried to be polite and said please and thank you for everything and couldn't stand up straight, she looked like the Tower of Pisa, even when she walked straight it looked as if she was leaning, she hardly lifted her feet from the floor, she did everything very very slowly, and everybody said softly this time it looks as if she's alright, because what else could they say? They sent her there, there was no changing that, so at least they could say that it was worth it, and when they felt that saying that it was worth it was a bit much, they said that it was necessary.

Translated from Hebrew by Dalya Bilu

DO *Kh.*

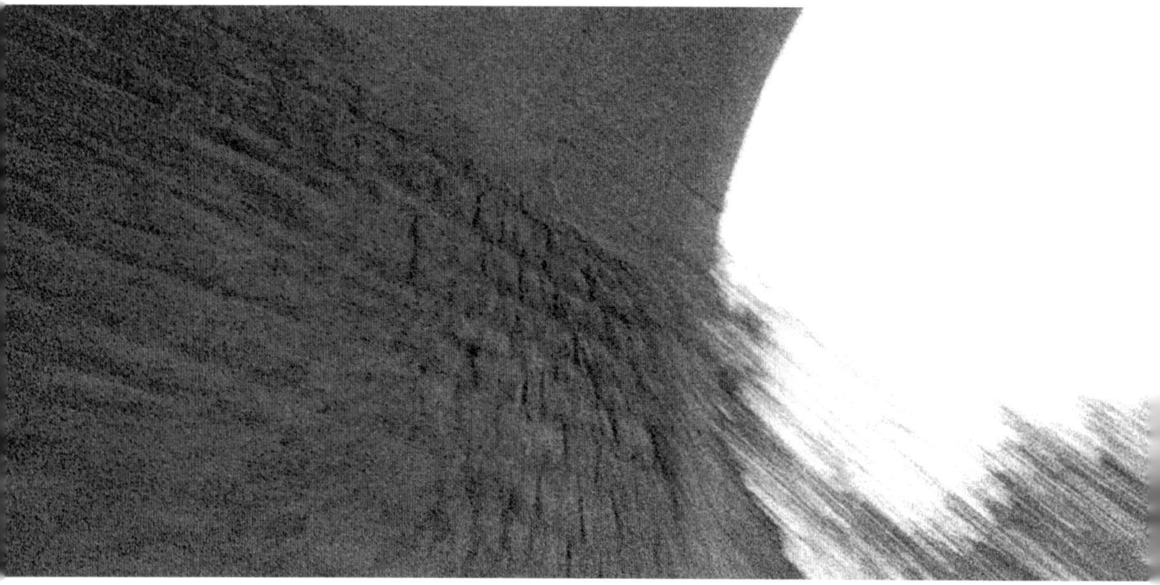

You Should Have Brought Flowers

Nhân doesn't know why he stops in front of the elevator. He stands there, hesitating for a few seconds, watches the door close. "It's probably the right elevator," he thinks. All the same, he goes back to the lobby to make a call on the in-house phone.

It's lunchtime. People are all dressed up, they gather in groups of five or seven. Nhân dials the number of the room he has just jotted on the slip of paper in his hand. At the other end of the line, a distant "hello."

"It's me," Nhân replies quickly.

"Where are you?"

"Downstairs. I just arrived."

"Why don't you come up."

"Room 748, right?" asks Nhân for no reason, staring at the slip of paper in his hand. Sheraton, room 748. He tries to prolong the moment.

"You see, I'm resourceful. I found it right away and here I am."

He wants to tell her that he ran here, jumped in the metro, just two stations, that now he's here, right downstairs, see... The voice on the other end of the line is impatient.

"Come on up."

"Okay, I'm coming."

Nhân hangs up the phone. Steady now, calm down. 748. All around him, people mill about, some with briefcases full of documents, others with cameras; they line up for the restaurant, rush toward the door. He runs back to the elevator.

He can't quite believe it yet. He stops again, anxious, in front of the elevator door, and then enters. Seventh floor. He follows the arrows, odd numbers, even numbers, pushes aside the fire doors, avoids the room service trays on the floor. Some have a solitary cup of coffee, others an empty champagne bottle upside down in a bucket, two smudged glasses. Two glasses. How touching. The door to room 748 is ajar, Quyên is waiting for him.

She steps back, gliding as if by magic to the back of the room.

Nhân shuts the door behind him. The room is huge, windows line an entire wall, they must look out onto something, but the curtains are drawn, all the lights are on – the ceiling, the head of the bed, the armchair, the table, the bathroom. A small suitcase lies open on the bed nearest him. On the other one, at the back of the room, Quyên is stretched out diagonally, her legs crossed. She lies facing the blank screen of the television.

Nhân moves toward her, glancing around the room. Out of the corner of his eye he takes it all in: two English-style bird prints on one wall, a huge glittering mirror over the dressing table, a breakfast tray littered with croissant crumbs, a US dollar tip. Nhân fumbles for the coffee pot. Quyên produces a cup out of nowhere.

"I kept it for you."

Another miracle. Quyên likes magic. Quyên glides magically to the back of the room, Quyên flies suddenly into the air and lands on the bed with her legs crossed, Quyên pulls a cup of coffee out of the void. American coffee, that's a luxury here.

"Is it really you?"

Nhân asks the question to reassure himself. Her apparition here is the greatest miracle of all. The armchair is too far away, Nhân sits on the floor.

"I'm swimming in luxury, don't you think?" Quyên says.

Luxury, but of course, the Sheraton Hotel, seventh floor, the dollar tip. He'll never get used to Quyên's miracles, to say nothing of luxury. Quyên has always been afraid of lacking luxury. He looks over at her.

Quyên squeezes an ashtray toward herself, she's smoking, she is carefully made up, but her hair is tangled, hasn't been combed. Quyên wears big curvy eyeglasses. Quyên has thick eyebrows. Quyên wears stonewashed jeans, Reebok sneakers, a thin ivory-colored silk blouse, sleeveless, showing her armpits. Quyên has big breasts pushed up by her bra.

"Have you been awake long?"

Quyên nods.

"You been out yet?"

Quyên shakes her head.

"I stayed in, tried to reach you by phone."

"But you're all dressed..."

"Well, I got up. I've got to get dressed... I wasn't sure I'd find you."

"You'd go out to find a lover."

Quyên groans. Nhân scrutinizes the room like a detective, there isn't a trace. She must have been alone last night. Nhân stares at the carpet for a minute, then looks at Quyên.

Quyên smiles slightly, almost maliciously, victorious: "I told you, wherever you go, one day I'll find you."

Nhân remembers Quyên's threats. And now, she's right, she's kept her word, she's scored a point. I know that she has magical powers.

Quyên scores a point, he doesn't give a damn. He forced her to look for him, she must have gotten impatient... He's not afraid, in fact, he's pleased.

"Bravo, sweetheart..."

Nhân is dazzled. "And you're very beautiful," he continues.

Quyên *is* beautiful. Quyên spreads out, catlike, like a woman in a pin-up calendar, Quyên glows like a three-dimensional image. Quyên shivers, quickly, as if illuminated by a violent film. Quyên is motionless, but Quyên is alive. Quyên is here, lying down, filling space with her luminous shapes.

"You're as beautiful as a Hong Kong starlet." He can't help saying it.

Quyên laughs. "I knew you'd say that."

No witchcraft about that, they're in Hong Kong.

Quyên is lying down, he's seated on the floor, in a room at the Sheraton Hotel, Nathan Road, corner of Salisbury Street, the Kowloon side of the city.

When Quyên called him, Nhân was stunned. He hadn't seen her in over a year. From time to time, a few words over the phone, long distance, some news, from farther and farther away, a few words on the back of brightly colored postcards, I'm here, I'm there, in the hotel on the card.

Nhân had been having a late breakfast, lingering over his coffee, when they paged him to come to the phone. "I'm in Hong Kong," she said. He jumped. He had just arrived in Hong Kong ten days ago, how did Quyên know, how did she find him? "I was informed..." Two or three phone calls to the United States, France, she explained, just like in a novel. I found out just like that. Like in a novel, romantic, dramatic. Nhân's hotel was called The Royal Bangkok, Pilken Street, in Hong Kong, he had been in the café on the ground floor bar with a friend, and suddenly a Vietnamese woman tells him tenderly, "Hey, it's me, your little sister."

"I'm only in Hong Kong for one night. Last night, I couldn't find you, I have to leave tonight, will you come, now?"

Why not, the Sheraton is close to the ferry pier. "Someone called me, a crazy story, I've got to leave," Nhân tells his friend. The guy was surprised. Nhân just vanished. I'm just a Don Juan, that's my fate. I'm spoiled, crazy things happen to me, but they're real. In a city filled with Chinese, God knows where they all come from, and after a year of separation Quyên calls him. *Quyên.* She's at the other end of Nathan Road. It's too complicated to tell it all from the start, where and why he and Quyên met, like in some cheap unbelievable spy film, all you need to know is that he ran until he was gasping for breath and that now Quyên is sprawled on the bed and he's on the floor in a room with the curtains drawn and we don't even know if there's a view onto the hotel's multi-story parking lot or onto Victoria Harbor. Really, it's like out of one of those television soaps, with the cloying muzak in the background. Nhân watches Quyên, you couldn't ask for more from three hours of videos. Nothing more beautiful, Quyên is a real woman, but Quyên glows. Quyên just stepped out of a video to lie down on this bed. He's lucky to be here, at her feet. Quyên is light, Quyên is a female Buddha, one of the most likeable, she doesn't resort to futile sermons. Quyên, the movie star, he doesn't ask for her autograph, he reaches out and clasps her ankle.

Love story.

Like in a film he saw as a kid, with Lê Quynh running down the hotel's corridors, Hong Kong teems with spies, jewels. Nhân is Z28, the Vietnamese Sean Connery. It's been more than ten years now that they've been abroad. What if…

"You look like a general's concubine," says Nhân.

Generals' concubines came here to swap currencies, deputies' wives to speculate on gold. It's been more than ten years now, Quyên's husband would probably have become the CEO of a few companies, he would ride around in a Honda, his exhausted face hidden behind the curtains of a car that the police would nod to under the Saigon sun. Quyên had come to Hong Kong to buy jade jewelry with the help of the Consul's wife, then she would go to Japan, the Ambassador's wife would take her to buy pearls and hi-fis.

"No, I mean it."

You committed adultery in Hong Kong, I would have gone back to Vietnam, your husband would have learned about it, he would have thrown me in prison, locked me in the zoo. What if… no, ten years already, what if… who can say, if he hadn't risen in the ranks, we might have trysted in Vung Tau, or Dalat, we would have fed the rumor mill, we'd have met each other secretly in Hong Kong, Nhân in the diplomatic corps, for example, Nhân in a black Peugeot 404, Nhân as attaché at the Vietnamese consulate.

And Quyên, the beautiful, the luxuriant. He takes off her shoes.

Quyên refusing to be the Chinese starlet.

Quyên refusing to be a Nationalist general's concubine.

Quyên refusing to be Madame Deputy. Nhân undoes the copper button of her jeans.

"You could play the whore," he proposes.

When Susie Wong was in Wanchai, in the black-and-white films, she had painted eyebrows and wore skirts slit all the way up to the thigh. She solicited night and day in a nightie in a brassy neon-lit bar on Hankow Street, not far from here. Quyên is slightly hurt, naturally she refuses to play the whore, she lifts her ass so he can pull off her jeans.

Nhân looks at the lace panties hiked up around her thighs, the hollow of her stomach under the sleek ivory satin, her short sporty white socks still hugging her feet and ankles.

"You should be naked, with a flowered veil hanging from a thread," says Nhân, cajoling. "Okay, you're not a whore, so why are you so difficult, you refuse everything…"

"I'm me," says Quyên, bending her legs so he can pull off her socks.

It's been more than ten years now. What if… They could have…

"Whatever had happened, I'd have gone abroad to study. Whether we had lost the country or not, I would have done this work, here, anyway," says Quyên.

"So the company pays the hotel bills, and lets you flit around, Hong Kong, Japan…?"

Quyên nods.

Nhân wraps his arms around her waist, pulls her to him. He presses a cheek to her breast, ponders the stray hairs in her armpits.

"You don't like the past. If things hadn't changed, today you'd be a *grande dame*."

"Well, Lady Doc, just because I'm a doctor's wife."

Quyên pouts.

Once upon a time, being a doctor was being somebody.

Doctor, Lady Doc? Nowadays, a doctor knows at best how to cure the hundred illnesses of men, women, old people, and children, he practices cosmetic surgery financed by insurance. Once upon a time in our country, a doctor was a learned man, the model of the idealistic intellectual, he knew how to compose beautiful poems, well-crafted essays, he wrote out his prescriptions with one hand and strummed the zither with the other, he guided the people, he governed the country, he changed the world, you really don't have much luck.

"Stop saying hurtful things," says Quyên.

And there wasn't just Quyên's husband. There was her father too. Nhân remembers a photo, Quyên wore pajamas, her father leaned against a Black Falcon, laughing, her mother wore an *ao zai* trimmed with sequins, a gold necklace. Happiness: a Falcon with air conditioning and a sticker on the window authorizing them to drive during curfew. Quyên in pajamas, the war rumbling in the background, General Nguyen Khanh outlawed the enemy, then one day a helicopter landed on the roof, she emigrated, and now she's perched on a bed in Hong Kong with only her underwear on.

But Quyên's happy, Quyên hasn't lost anything, the Falcon was replaced by an Audi 5000 with an automatically adjustable seat, her underwear is 65% polyester but has a Dior tag on the back. Sheraton. Would she have worn Guess jeans to visit the Consul? And the Perry Ellis bag. No, she hasn't lost a thing.

What was lost, who lost? Nhân looks at her in the mirror facing the bed.

He gropes to unbutton her shirt. "In my hotel, there's a Chinese waitress..." Nhân sucks one of Quyên's nipples, licks the arch of her breasts.

"She's not bad. She must still be in high school, speaks fluent English. The other day, when I ordered breakfast, she corrected me. I order eggs under easy and she asks me 'You mean, over easy?' What do I know? Over, under, it's all the same, a plate of eggs for English breakfast, there's no school for that."

"Scrambled, poached, sunny side up..." Quyên recites.

"That's easy, other things are more complicated."

Quyên agrees.

"You got her into bed?" Quyên asks.

"Into bed? I couldn't even order breakfast from her! I was blushing. Now I just copy the Chinese guys and order a bowl of rice *congee*..."

Nhân gets undressed, stretches out on Quyên. Comfortable, he sucks Quyên's nipple in and out, Quyen stares at the ceiling.

"I thought you could charm anybody..."

"Only you would be silly enough to believe that. You'd never guess, but when I miss you, I buy magazines of naked Chinese women."

Quyên laughs. *HK 97*, they sell it on the streets wrapped in clear plastic, impossible to flip through it just standing there, you've got to pay, bring it back to your room and unwrap it. Nhân tells it like it is: twenty Hong Kong dollars a copy, four different women, in various positions, glistening Chinese women, up close they almost resemble Quyên, fresh flesh, tender skin. This city is tolerant, but there are limits. So-called "artistic nudes" glitter under colored lights, against fake landscapes, just a hint of flesh between the legs.

Nhân pulls off Quyên's panties.

He studies the thick mound of hair at the base of her stomach, nuzzles his head in it, caresses her. He searches with his lips for the crack, the shuddering button of flesh. Nhân pulls back, gazes intently at the opening to Quyên's body. He examines it up close, fondles the folds at the base of her thighs, darts his tongue into the wet flesh.

The salty gluey flavor fades, her flesh swells to his touch. Nhân strays from Quyên's stomach, strains for her mouth. Quyên darts her tongue into his, feverish.

Nhân stretches out next to Quyên, moves his finger inside her. "I've missed you, inside, you know. You can get pleasure fucking anyone, but I miss the sticky soft inside of you..."

Quyên nods, as if to encourage him. Nhân, more daring, "I like to fuck you, do you like to fuck me."

"I like it..." Quyên pants.

"You like it..."

Quyên nods again, closing her eyes. No one watching him. Nhân hesitates, then he dares,

"I like your cunt..."

The word is only vulgar for an instant. Nhân lets the vulgarity fade, keeps the tenderness. The word cunt flows softly into his ears, this cunt that he tenderly fingers, that he searches tenderly, blindly, wall of soft flesh, above, below.

"I like the way your cunt hugs my dick, I like to feel my dick inside..."

Quyên nods, reaches to wrap her arms around his neck, pulls him toward her. Quyên arches her back, raises her legs, presses her lips against his, searching his mouth with her tongue.

Nhân falls onto the bed, his wet underwear bothers him. He doesn't have a condom with him. He ran over here, anyway where the hell do you find them in Hong Kong? If Quyên was a prostitute, there would be no problem, she would have this tool of the trade close at hand, otherwise Nhân would have complained. "Why didn't you get your husband to give you a prescription?" The question was more petty, vulgar, than the word cunt or dick. Cunt and dick sound good to the ear, but you're not going to say, "My male organ likes being in your female organ." Nhân's male organ really wants it, but he has no condom.

Quyên gets up. She slips her hand into Nhân's underwear, leans over, brings her head closer.

Nhân stops her with his arm, pulls her onto his body, hugs her to him.

This time, like all the others before, Quyên doesn't reach her goal. She's never come, not all the way. Quyên just says, "I'm like that." Nhân never understands her explanations, only senses somehow that she doesn't need to go all the way, that this pleasure is enough for her. "Naturally, that makes me happy. I like making love with you, why else would I do it, right off, every time I see you? It's just that I don't come, ever, that's all." Oh.

Nhân, sentimental: "Do you miss me?"

"Of course I miss you. Why else would I have come all this way, to look for you, in Hong Kong?

"But you're here on business."

"Business or no business, I looked for you."

"But I'm not avoiding you. I miss your cunt."

The word cunt has become familiar in his mouth. Quyên doesn't reproach him, but Nhân needs to explain.

"It's been a long time. I miss your cunt. I fuck around, but it's what I miss. Of course, I get pleasure, but I miss your cunt."

Quyên pouts.

"Let me kiss it again," Nhân whispers. "I love your cunt, I'll never get tired of kissing it."

Quyên accepts. Nhân turns her over. He kisses her back from top to bottom, squeezes the cheeks of her ass, spreads them. Quyên's cheeks are smooth, like the curves of a fruit. Nhân splits them, licking the folds of flesh nestled in the curly hairs.

It's been more than ten years now. Nothing is lost. Two Vietnamese, still fucking in a hotel in Hong Kong.

So far, it's been dramatic. It would be better in the United States. In the States, or in France, it would be just as dramatic. Big hotels look the same all over the world. You open the door to a room on the seventh floor in Hong Kong, you run in circles for awhile, you get lost on the fifth floor in Abidjan, on the ninth floor in Curaçao, Sheraton, Hyatt, stopovers in the airports. Lobbies at the entrance, at the exit restaurants, luxury shops, and bars. In Hong Kong or anywhere else. Here, there's a bar under the roof, on the highest floor, it's called The Great Wall, to be authentic.

Quyên says: "Last night, I went up there, watched the lights on the mainland. Just like the view from Victoria Peak, but without having to take the funicular."

"You went up there for a drink, all alone?"

"Of course, I'm a grownup, you know," says Quyên. "They had a Filipino band. I chatted with a few businessmen."

"Your laugh must have turned them on," says Nhân, stroking Quyên's hair.

"Guys away from their wives, looking for a good time..." Quyên pauses. "I came back to my room alone."

"What a shame... I didn't know you were here. Last night I went to the market for soup with a French friend. I brought some longans back to the hotel, lay down and watched a kung fu film on television. Every night, they've got kung fu films. Fight scenes from start to finish. I fall asleep after one film and a half. When I'm really anxious, I watch two of them. See how boring my life is?"

Nhân plays the martyr, begs a little tenderness.

I don't have what it takes to hang out in bars. My room is tiny, the window looks right into the next room, the only view is of clothes hung out to dry. I've stared out that window all the time, but I've yet to see a women undress and parade around. Now that would be a sight for sore eyes.

He gazes at the drawer of the bedside table. Inside, no doubt, is an American Bible, a gift of the Gideon Society. Probably. But certainly no condom for the traveler in need.

Nhân says, "My room only costs three hundred Hong Kong dollars a day."

"I don't pay for my room. I'm not hanging around like you. I'm here on business."

Quyên gets up, goes into the bathroom.

Nhân glances at the drawer, hesitates, but doesn't have the courage to open it.

The taxi dispatcher sputters in Cantonese, gibberish, incomprehensible, Nhân hears some names of battles, the Vietnam War, the invasion of Cambodia, *Tomorong, Dakto, Krek, Snoul…* Hey, snap out of it. "Kai Tak," he tells the cab driver. The Great Wall recedes in the distance, abandoned, Quyên had a drink there just yesterday. Ned Kelly's Last Stand, the jazz club a few streets away, that desperate night, he played the macho man, blasé. *Crazy wind over Khe Sanh, the afternoon.* Just to be sure, he says "airport" to the driver. The driver says, "OK, OK," acknowledging the command. Quyên is silent, snuggles closer to him. Bars with lewd names. Bottoms Up, that means ass in the air, nothing more exciting, Chinese girls waiting inside, faded flowers. *White nights in Laos.* Quyên came, she stayed with him for five hours in Hong Kong. *Suddenly, I'm alone, alone,* a corpse on some deserted battlefield.

Nhân takes Quyên to the airport, Nhân is not wearing camouflage and he doesn't carry an assault rifle. Nhân watches Quyên walk up to the Business Class check-in. In a moment, she'll be in a big armchair, a glass of champagne in her hand. Madame Vice Minister. More than ten years have gone by, otherwise, who would we have become? Has it all been a mistake? Suddenly, he asks her in a low voice,

"Quyên, I was so vulgar, are you mad at me?"

"No, it turned me on," Quyên replies in a loud voice in English. Nhân looks around, uneasy. *No, it turned me on,* in English, in public, lower your voice. Don't you know how to speak in Vietnamese anymore or what, Quyên. Nhân blushes. Like a schoolboy, he takes Quyên's hand.

No, it hasn't all been a mistake, it's rather pleasant. Today is much better than yesterday. He caresses her, feels how attached he is to her. Two lovers on the verge of separation. Quyên is very dignified in her dress, with her hair well combed. Nhân pretends to brood.

"What if I went back to Vietnam..."

Quyên looks at him, surprised.

"Not as a tourist. To stay..."

"Even as a tourist, I wouldn't go back," Quyên says firmly.

"I would rot there, I couldn't do anything. From time to time, out of charity, you would send me gifts, I would sell them in the street to make ends meet, which wouldn't be a problem, since you would keep me well supplied." He leans his head against her shoulder. "Yes, I'm just a parasite. But I'd be happy, you'd send me gifts."

Two lovers on the verge of separation.

Quyên is resolved, he knows it. Her grandparents served the French, her parents the Americans. Quyên followed the boat people to the West, Quyên is caustic, he teases her a bit. Quyên is Vietnamese, he should talk about the motherland when they see each other.

Quyên says: "If you go back to Vietnam, I won't need to feed you. You'll find a woman to take care of you."

Nhân bursts out laughing. It's true, he thinks. But he continues to plead with her. "You could at least send me some medicine, my wife would sell it at the flea market. So you would be acting nobly, a faithful lover."

"Oh, I'd feed you without any trouble, even if you stayed here," says Quyên, ending the conversation for the sake of appearances. Quyên doesn't care about the motherland. Quyên sticks to her opinions. Nhân feels like continuing his role in the little comedy he has invented.

It goes like this:

Suddenly, he sees Quyên again after a year of separation, or a bit less. She comes back. She hasn't changed. A random relationship, going nowhere. No real home, a few hours in a hotel room by accident, and after all they aren't going to commit double suicide by swallowing poison together. Nhân doesn't know what there is to regret.

Two lovers on the verge of separation.

"You should have brought flowers," says a middle-aged American woman, facing them.

Flowers? Nhân doesn't get it.

The woman continues: "You should have brought flowers, to wish her a good trip."

Quyên snaps at the woman in English.

Why, for no reason, does someone think they can come and harass you like that? Nhân stutters, embarrassed. In Hong Kong, where would you find flowers? It's like condoms, you never know where to find them. The woman is teasing him, his face must look pitiful. They must have let themselves get sentimental, Nhân thinks. Did she also hear Quyên say, "It turned me on"?

The woman insists, "You may not know it, but all you need are flowers to get through a difficult phase."

Nhân looks at the woman's hands and nods, for the sake of appearances. Quyên laughs, pleased, complicitous. What the hell is a difficult phase? They're émigrés, boat people, the earth's rotation makes them dizzy, they can't seem to make their way back home. It's been more than ten years now. If everything had continued like before, where would Nhân be, where would Quyên be, what would have become of them? The past has been severed so it'll never be the past again, today, that's it, all there is, they embrace, heartbroken, in a waiting room at Kai Tak airport, before she goes through the metal detectors, security, in a waiting room, while some American gives them a lesson.

Nhân's little comedy hasn't held up very well.

In the Sheraton Hotel, in Hong Kong, Quyên had gone along for the sake of appearances. I missed you, so I looked for you, we had a few hours to love each other, no more than the last time. So why ramble on, imagine that nothing's changed, that today you could bring it all back. A hotel room with the curtains drawn, you find them all over, we embrace, for a moment. But you and I, we're Vietnamese, you mumble obscenities in our mother tongue, the language of our ancestors, and it turns me on, what the hell is being Vietnamese anyway? And now I'm getting on a plane, you forget to offer me flowers, civilities, and they mock you.

A bunch of flowers, a difficult phase.

It's been more than ten years now, that's enough, isn't it. Either Quyên exists only in the moment, or Quyên only has a few hours for tenderness, she too is aloof. Life changes, people too. If only…

Nhân replies in clichés. To the American woman, vaguely to everyone, he says, "See you next time."

Translated from Vietnamese by Phan Huy Duong and Nina McPherson

Joost
ZWAGERMAN

How had Iris put it? *Sidney has clocked up an average of approximately four escapades a year.* Iris had been married to him for five years, so he must have gone through about twenty affairs during their marriage. How often would he have done it with each of those women? Theo decided on an average of twenty times per mistress. That added up to four hundred extramarital fucks for Sidney, and with a chance of, say, one in a hundred of infection, that was a considerable risk factor, for Iris, for him, for Sylvia...

Theo couldn't help it, couldn't stop these provisional calculations of probability from running through his mind. Even before he'd left Hoorn, the fear of disease and infection had returned and nestled in his belly.

It was past three, as always he had taken the route back via Heerhugowaard, the clouds had drifted away, from the middle of a clear blue sky the sun glared down on the windshield of his Toyota. Two paperclips on the dashboard flashed in a beam of piercing sunlight, and Theo's eyes shot back and forth between the road and the dash. An empty glasses case on the rear shelf behind him rustled back and forth constantly and ticked against the rear window every time he accelerated or changed direction...

He tried to think of something else and calmed down when he remembered the first weeks of Iris' appointment, now almost two years ago, the few moments in which he'd been able to make contact with her, between lessons, on sports days and parent-teacher evenings and of course that one all-important time in the gym when he'd had to deliver a small sticker-covered case containing an inhaler and two strips of Ventolin tablets which a mildly asthmatic first year had accidentally left behind in his classroom.

Decisively he sets off after the child. He's just checked the schedule and found out that the first year class has gym. He hurries through the corridors, reaches the gym via the boys' locker rooms, knocks softly on the door, no answer, he opens it hesitantly, and there she is, with her back to him, amid the twelve- and thirteen-year-olds whose spindly legs protrude from garish gym outfits. They're holding wooden hoops and have just raised them above their heads in imitation of Miss Pompier.

Loudly, her voice shrill and rasping, warm and husky, she gives her instructions – "and *stretch* your arms, and *bend* to the side" – and Theo feels his legs go wobbly beneath him. It's her diction, at first as despotic and compelling as the gym teachers' voices he remembers from his own school days, but then with something festive sounding through in the tight rhythm of her sentences. The children wave and turn their hoops. Nobody seems to have noticed him standing there enraptured in the doorway. Then Iris puts her hoop down on the floor beside her and ends the exercise by clapping three times. Two girls point him out. Iris turns and gives him a friendly questioning look. Theo gestures sluggishly with the case. The child scurries toward him, knock-kneed and quick, and reclaims it. Iris resumes the exercises without having to call the class to order, and before Theo closes the door he feasts his eyes one last time on her straight back, her sneakers, her black plait jerking side to side over the hood of her sweatshirt, the legs of her track suit tightened at the ankles with Velcro.

He floated through the corridors on his way back to his classroom, then spent the rest of the day trying to teach through a haze of emotion. Theo the Timorous, the mumbling sourpuss whose cynical remarks only appealed to the fifth and sixth years, whose appearance and manner inspired nothing but ridicule among the younger students, that day he let all the taunts pass him by. Half-dazed he hurried through his lessons, and now and then he felt his nostrils involuntarily flaring, caught up by the smells of the gym which seemed to have clung to him and followed him back to the classroom. Oh, the rubbery smell of the green linoleum, the leather of the horses and the basketballs packed away in the supply cupboard, the long mat which gave off a mixture of mothballs, unwashed hair, and plastic as soon as it was rolled out, and, through it all, the slightly addictive perfume of magnesium powder, floating through the room like pollen or gathering in little clumps in the creases of your palms after you've rubbed them in before climbing the ropes or doing a bird's nest or handstand on the rings. He had always associated these smells with the interminable gym lessons of his childhood, but the instant his gaze fell upon Iris they became inextricably bound to her presence. Months into their affair, there was still at least one moment every Tuesday afternoon when Theo discovered a slight scent of gym on her, even though she really smelled completely different, of walnut oil and dew-covered earth deep in the woods. Her body smelled lovely and exciting, that was undeniable, but all through their affair the smells which triggered the most intense images of their shared Tuesday afternoons were those of the gym. If he missed her over the weekend or during the holidays, all he had to do was summon up the chemical smell of the varnish on the long wooden benches that lined the walls of the gym and a mixture of scenes would tumble out, scenes in which Iris appeared, observed from points of view he had never actually occupied but was able to conjure up with such clarity that it was as if he had watched himself from a distance during their lovemaking purely for the benefit of future memory.

Sometimes it happened to him the other way around and he would be taken by surprise by a smell that had a remote similarity to the perfume of the gym. The smell of immaculate sporting articles in a department store could catapult him back to a series of impassively obscene scenes of himself in action with Iris at her house. Showers were compulsory after gym, so for an hour afterward his classroom was filled with a fresh smell of soap, shampoo, and wet hair, with as unavoidable side-effect the well-known locker room stench of dirty socks, musty shirts, and unwashed jeans. Of course, he had to be careful not to let things get out of hand. Once, he had waited till the end of the school day, when the building was almost deserted and the only people around were janitors or students on detention, and had slipped into one of the three gyms in order to refresh his olfactory memory. Odd, he knew it. Sometimes his fixation began to glide off into the realms of perversion. Sniffing at the pine cupboards in his own kitchen, for example, in the hope of recognizing the wooden smell of the batons, hoops, and pins. Or lifting the lid of the laundry basket in their bathroom late at night in order to gauge their own dirty washing and find out if it smelled just as sour and briny as Iris' gym clothes did after she'd taught in them all morning...

Theo forced himself to think of other things. He gripped the steering wheel. They shouldn't have parted like that, it should have been better, more beautiful. She'd gotten rid of him like a wet dog shaking the drops out of its coat. He clenched his teeth.

He reached down to the buttons of the car radio, hit the automatic search, let it pass a number of stations, stopped it at the twenty-four-hour one that played hits from the seventies, and sang along with the first number, loud, off the beat, half an octave too low. The side window was halfway down, the speakers boomed at full volume, he sang so loudly that the motorists he overtook gave him sideways glances, one of them even tapping out a furious staccato on his forehead the way Theo himself sometimes did when other drivers swerved past him too abruptly. By the time he reached Sint Pancras it was over. The song had ended and Theo's throat was raw. Singing at the top of your lungs was a relief, an exalted form of crying.

At home it turned out that Sylvia had gone into town. She'd left a note on the table. Beside it was a folder containing the instructions for the security system. A detector was attached just under the ceiling in one corner of the open-plan kitchen. It was a rectangular white box with a small window of frosted glass behind which Theo could make out two black bulbs like the spool knobs in a cassette recorder. The instructions claimed there were seven such detectors. Theo discovered more in the hall and laundry room and, yes, upstairs too. Theo combed the rooms of his own house as if it was a museum, with the instructions as his guide. There was a combination transmitter and a telephone alarm in the meter cabinet, two devices connected by a tangle of thin flat wires. A black siren the size of a telephone receiver was mounted on the back panel of the cupboard. With equal measures of respect and distaste, Theo studied it all. He should be feeling safe and protected, but instead he couldn't get away from the uneasy feeling that he had lost control over his own home to a closed circuit – he understood what it did but didn't know how to make it do it, despite having read the directions carefully. And he laughed out loud when he came to the flashing light described on the last page, *to be attached outside, preferably above the main entrance.* He went through the laundry room and the garage and came out in the front garden. It was true, a flashing light had been mounted above the front door. It made the whole front of the house look ridiculous, as if he was living in a village barracks or a grocery store. When he stood on tiptoe to see where the wiring went inside, he heard a voice behind him.

"Fantastic, isn't it?"

Caught red-handed, but at what? Theo turned around. Mrs. Does was standing next to the garden fence holding her bike. She was beaming.

"They installed it all in one day, in our house too," she said, pointing at the flashing light. "Your wife told me yesterday that she was going to call for a security system right away. So we did the same. And tomorrow they're going to that divorcée's down the road. She was scared half to death. No wonder, all alone with those two little kids."

Mrs. Does' smirk could only mean one thing, so Theo asked, "Heard anything else from the police?"

The joy which now broke through her beige foundation cream was completely genuine. "You won't believe it, but they've recovered it all. Every last thing!"

"Really?" asked Theo with enthusiasm.

"The police called first thing this morning with the good news. My husband went to the station right away. A fantastic coincidence, that's what the police said. Last night the police in Purmerend raided some, ummm, what do you call them?"

"Dealers?"

"That's it. And the things they found in the house, the police, it's beyond belief..." Mrs. Does shook her head and covered her mouth with her hand as if the Purmerend police had treated her to a personal tour. "It was jam packed with stolen goods. Even the bathrooms. TVs, car radios, computers, everything. And you know what was best of all? They only raided that house because of drugs and refugees. Or illegal immigrants, for all I know. What do you think of that?"

"Congratulations," he said. "What a stroke of luck."

"You can say that again. That's the first thing they said at the police station, they said, Mr. Does, they said, you are one very lucky man because the chance of recovering stolen goods in this day and age is minimal. Mi-ni-mal. It's incredible, isn't it? They just steal and rob and do whatever they like and nothing ever turns up again."

"Except this one time," said Theo.

Mrs. Does suddenly looked suspicious. She rested two fingers on her chin. "Wasn't that you out back this morning, in the parking lot? You looked like you were on a stakeout."

Caught after all. Theo tried to give her his most matter-of-fact smile.

"I was checking whether you could see the detectors from outside," he said.

"Oh, I see, of course," answered Mrs. Does, who clearly didn't believe him in the slightest. She could think whatever she liked as far as Theo was concerned, but unfortunately there was a chance of her buttonholing Sylvia about it. Gosh, I saw your husband out there in the parking lot all morning. Checking the security system, that's what he told me. Sylvia would be surprised enough that he hadn't been at school at that hour. When she heard what he'd been doing she'd think he'd gone totally mad.

Theo tried a long-winded excuse. He said that the apparatus shouldn't be visible from outside, because it's supposed to take the burglars by surprise.

"What about the flashing light?" asked Mrs. Does dryly. "The whole idea is for it to be visible. A flashing light like that is the perfect deterrent."

Of course he knew that as well as she did, but before he'd had a chance to answer, Mrs. Does returned to her solved burglary.

"You're not allowed to say so, but of course they turned out to be colored. Or at least some kind of foreigners anyway. It's an absolute scandal. If it was up to me I wouldn't think twice. Close the borders, no more family reunions, only let our Antillean cousins in once they've proved they work five days a week in a real job, and as far as all the illegal immigrants are concerned, straight to the airport with a one-way ticket back where they came from. You'd see, the country would be back on its feet in no time."

Theo noticed that she did it differently than his father-in-law had on Tuesday evening. The looks Mrs. Does was giving him had something triumphant and challenging about them. Once again he forced himself to smile. He gestured vaguely with one open hand and said, "That's how it is, Mrs. Does."

He added a polite nod, then opened the garage door.

Inside, he put the instructions back on the table. Neighbor, father-in-law, students, it was as if they were all doing it on purpose. He only had to step out his front door and certain remarks started flying toward him. He had to get rid of it. If he let it go any further he'd become a target for every racist who saw him as the ideal hypocrite, a walking excuse to finally let themselves go, because in their eyes he resented the very same things but just didn't have the guts to own up. From now on he'd keep his mouth shut, in the classroom, on the street, at his in-laws'. Where would protest and discussion get him? It was nothing but useless aggravation, wasted energy. And what was more, his moral indignation was thoroughly provincial. He had spent enough time at university in Amsterdam to know. In cities like Amsterdam, Rotterdam, and The Hague, integration and discrimination were practiced with more or less equal degrees of enthusiasm, plenty of racist insults and nicknames flying back and forth, but no one even raising an eyebrow at things like a black man passionately kissing a blonde girl in the back of the tram. The greatest misunderstanding of all was that nothing encouraged xenophobia more than poverty among ethnic minorities and the formation of ghettoes in old working-class neighborhoods. Success and prosperity caused just as much, if not more, aversion. If there was one thing that annoyed the Mrs. Doeses of this world more than a grimy rundown Turkish coffee house, it was a flashy and flourishing Turkish coffee house. Four young Moroccans racing through the streets in an old bomb were irksome; if they glided silently past in a brand-new four-door BMW, that was really something to get furious about.

Not that Theo had ever been big on rallying against injustice and wrongdoing. One step in a protest march was enough to have him lying on the asphalt in a phobic cramp gasping for breath. Was that his fault? He was simply unfit for active engagement. At most he was an expert in repugnance and reserve, even though he liked to keep theory and practice separate and applied his disgust to humanity as a whole, not to his fellow humans. In thought a solipsist, in deed a boy scout.

Perhaps this dichotomy explained the unfortunate outcome of his collision with Wouter Nijman. And Theo wondered if he himself hadn't made it turn nasty there in the classroom half on purpose, the perhaps inevitable consequence of a long-suppressed yearning for an untroubled existence, far from children and school.

To be achieved, if necessary, by means of suspension, reduced pay pending an investigation, notice of dismissal...

It was almost five. Through the kitchen window Theo watched the breadwinners rolling down the street in their dark blue Volvos, Peugeots, and Volkswagens. Children got off their mountain bikes and gaily rushed over to their fathers. Theo followed the scenes, aloof, unsure whether they should be consoling or annoying him. He drank a glass of water standing at the sink. Then he heard Sylvia arrive. He heard the three familiar clicks of the front door lock from the hallway and for a moment he hoped for a repetition of the euphoria that had overwhelmed him that afternoon when he had observed her from a distance. He even imagined her entering in a kind of cloud of redemption which would immediately sweep him up alongside her, but when she really came into the room, maneuvering awkwardly with three large paper bags from clothing stores, her pupils were constricted, her movements angular. She closed the door behind herself with an unusual ferocity. It was clear that something had happened earlier in the day, something she was blaming on him. Theo instantly feared one thing, the one thing he'd been constantly afraid of for the last fourteen months.

Sylvia put her bags down. She didn't return his greeting and avoided meeting his eyes when he asked if she wanted something to drink. She draped her coat over a chair and asked, "And how were things at school?"

His heart skipped a beat. Everything had come out.

When he didn't answer right away, she said, "There was a phone call for you this afternoon."

He felt as if his skin was being stretched taut in different places over his body.

"Oh? Who?"

Iris, who else? She had regretted her laconic goodbye. For the first time she hadn't been able to control herself and had called him up as soon as she'd arrived home, without stopping to think that he'd still be en route to Alkmaar. Stupid bitch. Right at the end she'd betrayed everything and ruined it all.

"Ferweda," said Sylvia. Now she did look at him, measuring his reaction. "He was surprised you weren't in. I was surprised you weren't at school."

For Theo these two sentences were so simple they almost sounded flippant. To his horror he felt a grin welling up.

"Something is escaping me," said Sylvia icily. "Perhaps I said something funny."

"No, no, not at all," he answered quickly.

"Theo, I don't appreciate being forced to act like the kind of woman who wants to know where her husband has been. That's beneath me."

She's practiced this part, he thought. She sounded as if she was about to close the case for the prosecution. But instead she said: "But all the same I want to know Where you've been."

He couldn't help it. Once again he had to struggle not to smile. He clamped his lips together, knowing that Sylvia would misinterpret his nervous grimace.

"I don't understand," she said. "Why weren't you at school? Where were you, Theo?"

Instead of sounding icy she now sounded sad and frightened. All at once, Theo felt his involuntary smirk disappear. More than anything, he wanted to kiss her.

"I can explain," he said, and wondered what he would say next and how much he was still able to keep back.

Translated from Dutch by David Colmer

Pierre *MARTORY*

Obscure Gestures

Those obscure gestures... of necessity forgotten...
as soon as they are made. —Michel Foucault

White space peopled with empty shapes.
I say: You. I see my blurred image
At the bottom of a drained glass.
Gold paillettes stars to die for
Or sun-umbrella of stratagems. My life.

The others joined together on the surface of things,
Flies that don't know they've always been dead
Ancient and nameless warriors.
Today I'm staggering. A drop of blood
Slid between the sky and me

Which will make me lose the image of the clouds
And think the rain will wash everything.
Tomorrow will no longer know what yesterday was
With its standing shadows its lost promises
In hallucinatory forests.

Groove after groove always beginning again
I talk like a gramophone
To the buried centuries. I'm trying to find which spiderweb
Has trapped my words –
Too brilliant insect borrowed elegance.

From a Private Domain

I'll go count my scattered flocks
Living allusion to my innumerable fathers
But how do I attain to the number of stars
Painted as far as the distant boundaries of space?

Out there, rivers flow away or circle back
Phantasms gifted with the sense of touch with perfume
They let you hope for a taste of ripe kisses
A regret a fallen apple or the rain.

Why inhale the delicious rot here,
Lift ancestral petticoats to discover,
Perhaps to regret, forgotten questions?

The domain is enclosed as far as we wish it,
To feel less alone in the nights remaining to us,
To see farther to distinguish other company.

Without Rhyme or Reason

after a poem by Eugene Richie

There's nothing but a book in a foreign language.
Somebody read it and shut it on the table,
Forgot it, went away.

Nothing but a bridge of vines that gets you to
A light an uninhabited savannah
Halfway through a towering abyss.

Nothing but laughter Chinese voices floating
Incomprehensible in the air the next day
Memory music torn to pieces forever.

Whoever you are keep an eye on the gorilla
In you drumming near your heart.
Have you really ever spoken to the one you love?

Everyone has gathered together in this station.
Outside the wind savagely ruffles the lake.
Will afternoon escape once more without us?

An almost full moon in sulfurous clouds
Rises behind the tree whose name will have to be invented.
Will the bugler playing taps settle our debt,

Or perhaps it's better to stay on one's mat, dreaming...

Oh, Lake...

Exquisite invasive fear just as night
Leaves the dozing cities and I wait,
Adorned like a bird lifting the sun,
For a new day to disentangle the clouds.

The hour passes and from her to me stretches
The deep warmth of our mouths
And I touch this corruptible flesh
She and I combustion soon to be rubbish

Everything passes she'll say (allusion to the poet).
The music distilled between us will no doubt return
To this obscene silence
We felt during self-centered sleep.

Then when the blood of so many wounds
Inflicted on our hearts dries on our eyes
We'll let the permanent night finish
Its slow work of destruction inside us...

I placed her in a mirrored coffin
To magnify the growing pallor of her features.

A reddish-purple ribbon to mourn the death of hope.

Ten Years for Example After

Ten years for example after the very day
Of the reflection of a large cloud in the branches
I'll have left the others at dusk
Because in my present state no one could have
Kept me without an apparent reason because
It was from now on precisely too late for me.

Others might have thought it's always too soon
To reach that dawn without suspecting anything
Not even being away ten years ten days ten centuries
So that these branches these clouds this reflection
Could no longer be in us who would no longer be here

It's hard to think that neither my eyes
Nor the smallest color in the world
Nor the word eye nor the word world will be nothing
Not to mention the dreams and the one heart that beats

Wait to be outside facing who knows what nothing
What unimaginable always never anybody
That you won't even be there to taste.

Translated from French by John Ashbery

Hong *YING*

The Dirty Finger on the Bottle Lid

They shut their eyes on purpose to prevent me from finding them. He came straight over from Mother's. "Your family's removed your name from the family tree." He shot out his hand to support the falling broom and picked up the old blue shirt that was perched on top.

"Well, go on!" I watched the gum roll around and around under his tongue. Saliva lapped at the edges of his lips.

"Your family's changed the position of the door to stop the ghosts from coming back."

"Ghosts? What ghosts?"

He went on. "They had a whole gang of workmen over to block up the original door. I went past the house several times that day. They were making the most terrible racket. It went on nearly all night."

I interrupted, forcing him to put the broom down. He took the piece of gum out of his mouth and kneaded it in his hand. First it was a person lying gleaming white in his palm. Then all at once it had been remolded. "It's a ball. No, it's a head." As I spoke, he shook his hand several times to get rid of the gum, but it had stuck fast to his palm.

I walked across, bent over, and gazed down at him for a minute at the foot of the steps. Then I stretched out my hand and grabbed hold of him, taking the white head between my thumb and forefinger and sticking it on the fence. Clapping my hands, I cocked my head to one side to indicate that he was to follow me.

He had an oval face with low flat temples. His hair was thinning on top. The lower corner of the mirror in front of the counter was decorated with scarlet petal shavings. I spotted him in the heaving crowd keeping his eyes firmly to himself. A piercing raucous sound burst from the orchestra. Wine glasses littered the windowsills, carpets, tables. Glass crunched above the rhythm of the music.

As I moved through the crowd and climbed the stairs, the din receded.

The curtains in the room were tightly drawn, a painted landscape of bright green trees, but gaps revealed glimpses of chimneys and cables. I went to the toilet, flushed, buttoned up my pants, opened the door. He was standing there gawking, unsure what to do with his hands and feet, his uncertainty in sharp contrast to his self-confident manner earlier.

I dug out my makeup purse, applied some lipstick, and instructed him to sit down.

"Where?" There were no chairs in the room, only a bed.

I pointed to a tall pile of old magazines and newspapers. He sat gingerly, placing his hands on either side of the pile to steady himself. I grinned.

"What's so funny?" He raised his head to look at me, his face registering annoyance.

I replaced the makeup purse in my handbag. "Look, I'm the one without a home to go to. What are you so afraid of? You could just as well take me as one of those tarts you pick up on the street."

That wasn't what he meant, he explained falteringly. Then he added, "I thought you'd already taken off."

"Taken off?" I repeated. "Oh, I see." I told him I thought everyone was prone to madness, he and I included. I squatted down. I could still hear people crying, crows cawing, dogs barking, pigs snorting, bleating sheep. His shoulders twitched. He buried his head in his lap. I stopped. I felt the untimely drawing-in of evening. It was just past six, yet the sky was already beginning to darken. The gaps in the curtains had gone. The room was lacquer-black. I pushed him onto the bed. I held him, whispering, "Don't cry, my poor soul. Then who'll come to your rescue tonight?"

I deliberately put myself to one side and let her appear.

Every time she appeared she was carrying a wine glass which contained cold water from the tap. "No, it isn't. It's wine. The cheapest wine available in the city. You can't beat the taste of poor quality wine, you know." As she spoke, she massaged her throat with her thumb and forefinger, forcing the wine back into her mouth before swallowing it in one gulp.

Outside, members of her family were moving about anxiously. She put the wine glass down and remained close to the table, not seeing the shadows of the people by the door. She seemed to be listening to something a long way off. She inclined her head toward the table, her hair falling forward and obscuring her burning face.

Her lips were unusually full, beautiful in a Western sort of way, singed by the alcohol. She reached out for the wine bottle, but it eluded her grasp, and she grunted quietly, rubbed her scalding cheeks with her hands, her disordered hair swinging loosely, flicked through the pile of books on the chair and then impulsively tossed them toward the window. But the pale yellow sun was just a reflection of the light. The books hit the pane and came thudding back to the floor like that bird that shot out of its wide airy exquisite cage merely to crash into the pane, leaving a shoal of blood.

She picked up half a photograph that was sticking out of one of the books. It was in black and white and slightly out of focus. It showed a young girl with a thin neck and unnaturally large round staring eyes. What was she so afraid of? Was it the windmill in the background decorated with little red flags? Yes, that was the day her older brother had opened the birdcage and bundled in the little bird with the gray head and black wings. Then after smothering the cage with a quilt, all of a sudden he had opened it.

This is unlucky, I kept reminding myself, although in truth I was not entirely clear as to why it was unlucky. In the two weeks since renting the apartment, I had been trying to figure out what I'd been doing prior to moving in, and where I'd been. The spider orchids and irises were flowering furiously in every corner, but ever since a giant drone stung me on the finger, I had become impervious to the attractions of scented flowers.

The lights were on in the theater. The repertoire was well known to me. The doors had clearly been open for some time, no one on duty, the foyer deserted. I walked in and sat in the back row.

As the curtain went up on the stage, a cat jumped down and scurried off into the audience. A song reverberated through the dark. My ears were ringing. I pressed down on my bee-stung finger and uncrossed my legs. The stage was swirling with snowflakes. Choruses of men and women wandered back and forth singing plaintive songs which struck a chord with me. The lights flashed. The curtain came down.

When the curtain went up again, a policeman was questioning a hunchback in a headscarf. "You're our main suspect. Tell me, please, when did you go into the restaurant? To the station? How long did it take you to get from the restaurant to the station?"

The hunchback moved from stage right onto the proscenium. She turned her face. It was badly wrinkled, as if covered with a net, but her eyes were bright. She held her hands in front of her chest, as if she was lost in memories that bore no relation to the policeman. The policeman told her she had no right to remain silent, that she was obliged to answer his questions. "It's the law," he barked.

A young woman sang a rousing tune.

I felt something gagging my mouth and my neck being stroked. I was immobilized. Then like a gust of wind something powerful took flight. I stood and, apologizing, edged my way toward the aisle and pushed open the emergency exit. When I reached the empty foyer the singing faded into silence. Even the toilet was devoid of smokers.

I left the theater through the glass doors and turned up my collar against the cold oncoming wind. A cat stood up on its hind legs and padded along the sidewalk behind me for a few meters. In the desolation of the night only the theater seemed to be brightly lit. Crossing the road, I negotiated a route around a white racing bicycle parked on the curb. Unconsciously, my hand reached out to touch the raindrops on the surface of the bike. They were unpleasantly cold. Suddenly, I understood the message in the song I had heard at the theater: the two of us must return to the day before, otherwise they wouldn't make it through the night.

Unless, unless.

The melodious voice paused. The violin, cello, and piano ensemble played on in the background. "Unless they can meet tonight," continued the song.

The cat's pace quickened to within a step behind me. I was lost in abstractions. My objectives were crumbling. I stopped at the foot of the cross by the entrance to the cemetery and turned my head toward the chiming church clock. Against the night sky all that remained of the theater's steep pitched roof was a triangular frame. Just then I saw his head appear at the theater window. He shouted to me asking me to slow down. He pointed to the fire escape outside the window. Did he want me to climb up?

I groped around for the switch by the door and put the light on. The cat covered its face. "Switch it off!" it said.

I flicked the switch and the light went out. The cat went straight over to the table and lit the candle. "That's more like it," the cat said. I shivered.

Suddenly the door opened. Yawning, I went over to close it. It needed shutting twice for it to stay closed. A person with an arched back was standing there. Forcing my eyelids open, I realized that this person was really a heap of clothes and hats hanging on the back of the door. I sensed the cat looking me up and down.

"You have a wonderful back," it said eventually.

I turned around and saw the cat sitting in my chair toying with a plaster cast of a face that I'd hung on my wall.

I took the face out of the cat's paws and replaced it on the wall. The cat was unusually large, its fur black and glossy all over, its claws long and sharp, its blue eyes piercing, lively, tender.

"Like some wine?" My voice was exquisitely husky.

The cat was curled up in the chair, flicking its tail. Its noncommittal attitude intrigued me. I poured myself a glass of port and raised it to my lips. The cat jumped down in front of me, snatched the glass and downed the port. It shook its head and handed back the glass. My eyes weren't deceiving me: the cat was rubbing the area between its legs.

There was a fumbling, a zipper being undone. I froze. The cat was pulling at a seam between its legs as if peeling off a skin. A man stepped out. He threw the cat skin over the chair.

The sound of splashing. I lay on the bed preparing to welcome the man when he came in. Before long the bathroom door opened. He emerged, a perfect naked male physique. In front of the mirror he pulled on the cat skin, leaving only his thing showing. He said it felt particularly good this way.

I rolled over on the bed, deliberately turning my back to him. I heard him padding around the room, pressing close to me, those light footsteps like a love song. I drew a deep breath. The flickering candlelight illuminated the mask on the wall, the furniture and the unlit light hanging in the middle. The chair began to creak. He was playing with himself. I sat up on the bed.

"Those poppies swaying in the wind aren't for the war dead. They're dedicated to you."

"I know."

"You came up the slope from the lane by the stream, looking at the view as you climbed. You must have seen the two of us, me and her."

He and I had been in bed all day. She came over. He let her lie down on his right. She was staring at me although my profile was obscured in part by him lying between us. She noticed my eyes wandering over the woodpile next to the stove and shifted her gaze in that direction. We were not meant to meet like this, she and I.

He had one protective arm around her and the other around me. It was some time before I noticed her pregnancy. He didn't seem bothered in the slightest. Immersed in his book, he didn't register that I'd gotten up and was mechanically going into various rooms carrying dishes for the meal and setting out our bowls and chopsticks. She remained there, clutching her belly. She was clearly wary of me. He turned the pages of his book, his eyes glued to the text.

"So is he the guy you met down by the river when the fog lifted?"

"Yes. I seem to be smoking more than ever. Do you want one?"

"Thank you, no. I gave up several years ago. Do you know what I think about you when I'm lying in his arms?"

"What?"

"Every morning when I get up to make his breakfast, I think that the girl by the side of the river is me. To be honest, in moments like those, I could happily murder you."

She was daydreaming when he pushed her toward the French windows. Her clothes fell to the floor. He exposed her large belly. Beyond the window an apartment house was under construction. Workmen, wolf-whistling youths, little groups of sightseers, punks in their regalia, all transfixed by her naked pregnant body. But he was not looking at her. He was facing the other way, watching me.

I stood with my legs apart and waited.

Thc phone rang. The doorbell. They opened their eyes as usual. "You'd better get a move on. There are too many of them waiting. If you hang on any longer, they'll be along, one by one."

"So in the end, having gone from city to city, you settled on this place?"

"I went to the mill." The market was dark and almost deserted. Old sofas, beds, books, and records were arranged on the floor for sale. In the street, a band was blasting out a tune. Gray pigeons flew in all directions. The music was like an incantation. I felt around in my pocket for some coins. They jumped around this way and that. I turned to face him standing on the half-rotted bridge.

The stream was the only clean thing left in the town. He listened and stuck out his tongue. "So you don't consider yourself dirty and disgusting, stinking to high heaven then?" he snorted.

He pounded the wooden posts with his fists as if he was beating at the heart of the city. My head spun with the sound of the thudding.

I knew I was playing a game. I never had a moment's peace, and that was the truth. I walked in the direction of the road at the head of the bridge.

Someone was calling my name. The voice was soft. I felt myself turn over and my legs curl up.

Don't be alarmed. I'm not. *Don't move.* I'm not. *Go to sleep.*

I watched the white plaster mask drop down onto the mirror.

This evening I once again fled to the streets. The wind was blowing in the oak trees. I closed my eyes for a moment. When I reopened them they were burning with invitation and desire.

There was a soccer game on the television in the bar but the wild roars made no impression on the chatter of men and women drinking.

"A gin and tonic, please." I placed my hands on the bar for support.

"Oh it's you."

I withdrew my hands. The bartender seemed surprised. "You haven't forgotten have you? That day I made you a special cocktail. At first you thought things were a bit quiet, but you said that if you were the waitress, business would definitely pick up. And you got cracking right away, taking off all your clothes until all you were wearing was a hat and a short skirt."

"Really?"

"Business was particularly good that day." He put ice cubes in the glass. "In the end you tied a bit of string around your leg to hold your earnings. You paraded up and down with the menu between your labia, showing the customers. You flaunted your body all around the room. I couldn't keep my eyes off you."

"Knock it off, would you? You filthy sex maniac!" I rapped on the bar to interrupt his lewd imaginings. But his description of these obscene and coquettish goings-on had unsettled me. I didn't get angry. When I finished my drink, I took some money out of my purse to pay him.

He refused. "Why don't you hang around for awhile? Have another, whatever you like."

"No thank you."

"It was definitely you. By the end of the evening all you had on were those parrot earrings."

I admitted to him that I'd been there. But this time I'd come in to meet someone. I seated myself next to the window, then I heard the sound of a gun. That was the end of business for that evening.

He looked at me, then lowered his head. I weaved my way through the noisy crowds. As I pushed open the door to the back of the bar, I took off my hat and gestured to him.

There was an empty stage. I was their only audience. They were asking each other questions, talking about things impossible to forget.

They'd grown beards. They carried on talking, their eyes crossing over me in a trance. I grew tired of listening to the saga of their love lives. What was I doing there? Their coarse smutty talk shattered my laughter. They were perplexed.

That was an opening. The aim was to keep it simple. From there, one could move on, to a 17th century castle, to a ceremony in some future century. Then I remembered my recapture the night before.

I was taken into the family dining room. All the female relatives on both sides were there. I asked my mother why I had been brought back when she had already agreed to my leaving.

The family cat edged its way past my feet, then ran to the foot of the bed to munch on a fishbone. My mother's voice was calm. "You have disgraced our family."

For the first time, I expressed with my eyes all the feelings about my mother I'd experienced all these years. My mother had never seen my eyes like this. Formidable. The bamboo bed we were sitting on collapsed. After everyone had propped mother in a chair, they lifted the board to find the cat underneath, bloody and squashed. A child screamed hysterically. An adult smacked it. The mess was cleared away. The two women next to my mother burst out laughing.

"What have you done with him?" I asked.

"Chopped off his you-know-what. It'll make a nice soup!"

My mother looked me up and down. "We didn't force you, you forced us." She paused. "The way you're earning your crust is no better than begging!" She hunted around in my bag for the manuscript, then tore it into pieces and flung them in my face. It was impossible to piece it back together again.

I picked up where my mother had left off. "I'm an embarrassment to your family because I'm lewd."

"Well you said it!" My mother looked at me and brushed me away with her hand. "Go! As far away as possible. Perhaps you'll find someone you'll be content with, someone you can settle down with." She added, "Then you may come back."

"Never." I stepped in a patch of cat's blood that had escaped the cleaning. Grabbing hold of the washstand, I wiped the sole of my shoe on the floor to remove all traces of blood.

Translated from Chinese by Jenny Putin

BEAR
Kirkpatrick

The King of the Dogs

Deke is reading the story in one of her magazines about night vision. We're eating brownies from the bakery, drinking milkshakes we made from a customer's blender. Deke finger flips the pages and then spits out some shake and holds up for me to see the picture of a man in the jungle with huge goggles strapped to his head. I'm just trying to stay still, trying to keep the dogs in me from going crazy or biting someone or just pissing anywhere.

She says, You know the place I'm talking about. Some fucking guy sitting on two fully stocked trout ponds. Fresh water pumped in, fences all around the joint.

She crosses her arms, the sinews in her tan forearms spidering.

She says, Pretty secure, safe.

My town is like this. The edges are slightly invisible, as if only the extraordinary happens at night or just after we turn our heads. Deke says we turn our heads a little quicker than most, especially the Unitarian crowd, which is almost all of us.

What I know is that some of us wait all day for the sun to go down.

Deke pulls the innards from Mrs. Wolfson's Electrolux vacuum cleaner, squints at the dusty wires for a moment, stuffs them into a trashcan. I've only been with her three days, since my mother answered the summer help wanted sign in the window for this new store in town. Now Deke gives me a few bucks, says, Go get us some pizza and cokes. Says she has some things on her mind, needs some fuel.

When I get back, Deke is thumbing through one of her magazines.

She says, We're going fishing one of these nights. Be like father and son. Sort of. Won't seem suspicious at all.

At night, I let a few of the dogs out of their fences, and we run in the fields outside of town, the legions of God's servants, the Wheelers' dog leading the way with her nose, taking us to the river. Sometimes the dogs stay away from me when I really juke and flop.

My mother says I need money to start buying my own pills for when I wake up, for when I go to bed, for just about any time in between, or find something that stops me from running in circles, swinging my arms around, going zigzag like a trout with a bang on the head. In two years I'll be driving a car, she says, got to have money, she says, got to have money to get a girlfriend.

Deke says that people don't even need a license to fish in that guy's place, but then he socks you by selling you the trout you caught by the pound. Deke is eyeing me as if this is the usual around here. She calls him that guy as if she's mad, but everyone in town knows his name, Mr. Leeder, used to teach at the high school.

Deke says, Vietnam vet, big deal.

Deke says, The shit we got these days, puts their sorry old men asses to shame.

At work Deke tells me about dust, starts me with vacuums.

Deke says, It's dust that kills these things.

She waves her hand like a benediction over the bodies of the old vacuum cleaners scattered around the workshop.

She says, All it is is dust, gets everywhere, starts clogging things, messing up connections. But tell me this, Mr. Eighth Grade, where do you think the dust comes from?

The whole time she's saying this she's eyeing the sausage sub in her hands, looking for the next place to bite, and when she's done talking she immediately stuffs about a third of it into her mouth, bites it off, eyes wild, then nods her head and chews methodically while she looks at me.

I want to go out back, what I do when I tell Deke I have to go to the bathroom.

She puts a big hand on her getting bigger thigh, says, So, give me an answer. Outer space? Corn fields? Dogs? Cats? Birds? Hm? All wrong. Dust is skin, kid.

She sticks out a tanned forearm and rubs it with her hand.

She says, You can't see it, but that's what it is. We're all falling apart, every day, inside and out, kid, inside and out.

I try as hard as I can to hold it in, but I can't. I book out the back door and start circling the piles of junk as fast as I can, zipping around the old washers, dryers, shop vacs, generators, throwing my head around as if to get the dust out the holes of my ears, noises I've never heard of wanting to come out of my mouth. I'm leaning into the corners, sending my feet out wide so when I bend into the turns I won't fall, but I can't go fast enough to get where I want to go. I can't get around the corners fast enough.

Deke tells me to meet her, back of the Unitarian cemetery, after the streetlights go off. I've been three weeks with Deke, learning about vacuum cleaners and the dust that ruins them all. Deke's been promising fishing at night, and I sometimes wonder if she hasn't been going already. Tonight, she says, meet her tonight. I wait in my room, hear the TV downstairs, the window open, the under the tongue pills spit out into the windowsill, the dirty clothes under the blanket in the shape of a sleeping boy, some cookies for Deke when she's thinking.

I wait, crouching under the windowsill, looking at the empty streets and the bugs under the yellowish lights, the Williams' house across the street, the only light inside casting gray and blue dark shadows on their windows.

Then the streetlights go off, and I'm out the window, sneaker crunching across the asphalt shingles, the rose bush whispering on the stepping down trellis.

Running to the shop in town, I jerk and buck, feeling my heart going like the Browns' crazy backyard dog, fenced in, shaking and jumping after just hearing its name, twisting, twisting.

Her shape sits on an overturned bucket, but the salami and mustard smell makes me believe it's her.

Deke says, Goddamn, kid. We ain't going to the moon. Here, have a bite of this, give you some ballast. You know what ballast is, kid? Chrissake, don't choke. You're weird, you know that kid, weird. Weirdest looking kid I ever saw. Eyes going all over, running around like some weird bird with sneakers and a dirty face. How come I never see you wash your face? Didn't I teach you anything in Sunday school?

Deke gives me the rest of the sandwich and I'm chewing as fast as a mouse.

Deke says, Kid, you think we'll get arrested? That's what they do with people who don't like what's going on, you know. They kick them out of their jobs, thinking the devil's in them.

Deke hands me wire cutters, shoulders a pack.

Deke says, Now on, no more talking.

I'm smiling in the dark so hard I feel it tingle my face, run around my neck, and I've got to pee but I hold it, and I follow Deke's back down the sidewalk of town, past the other stores, and turn left into the darkness of the cemetery, stones suddenly appearing in a glowing lean, the trees in back rising above, dark and still against the near dark summer sky, swallowing us. I follow the Deke noises, the leafy shush and mouth pant, out into a field, over a stone wall, across another field, mooneyed cows moving out of the way slow, then quick, as if their own movement frightens them more. Trees again, pressing off them silent with my hands pretending I can jump from one to another like a frog, then another field from where we can see a light on in a trailer below, a truck nearby, and just barely a dirt driveway that leads to the face of a darkened field with two black eyes of water, the surface a thick black wetness of summer sky blue at night.

I'm all over the place, running in circles, feeling my body tilt in toward a center that I can hold up with the speed and squeak of my feet. I wiggle my arms around, jiggle my head until my lips are flapping.

Deke sits down, I can see her go by again and again, slowly sitting down in freeze frame images like when you open and shut your eyes at cars going by your window at night. I see her messing around in her pack, and then I see her eating.

My thoughts are beginning to spin off kilter, leveling skyward until I fall on my back, breathing like a fish on the grass.

Deke says, A fruitcake, that's what you are.

I smell pastrami and pickles, hear drink gurgle from a canteen.

Deke says, Think about the Marine Corps, kid. You can run circles like that all day and night, dig yourself a hole right through the earth, come out the other side in the desert somewhere.

Deke's moving her hands over her arms, neck, face.

Deke says, Here, skeeter stuff. You never see these bastards during the day, do you kid?

Deke crawls on all fours and I follow. At the fence I hand Deke the wire cutters, but it looks short enough to climb. The light on in the trailer blinks when somebody walks across the window, back and forth, blink, blink. I blink my eyes when he's there, open them when he's not there, almost time it so I don't see him.

Deke's fingers make metal clinks, a swear from her mouth. She's got kind of a huge ass.

I want something to happen. I look upward and then swing my head back and forth like a dog with something bad in its mouth until I get so dizzy I have to close my eyes and rest my forehead on the grass. Then I imagine I'm hiding behind the huge assness of Deke, her protecting me from the silver black of the water's surface that makes my back shiver like a fish when I think of touching it.

Deke is through the fence, reaching back to pull her pack behind her, crawling to the pond, observing all discipline.

Close to the water we move slow, keeping the rustle of grass to our knees and toe pointed feet. We set up lines with bobbers, baiting our hooks with pieces of roast beef from one of Deke's sandwiches.

Deke whispers, Roast beef, ooohhh, they love it.

Then Deke starts eating the rest of the sandwich.

We're into trout, they're hitting heavy, the night feeders. Sharks, Deke calls them, out and willing. She tells me there are certain trout, something about their brain makeup, they only come out at night to feed. Deke's got six in her pack, and I forgot something to bring them in so I take off my t-shirt, wet it, then lay the fish side by side after Deke whacks them a few times on the forehead with her knife handle, their heads making a wet hollow sound.

Then, right out loud, Deke says, Hey kid, you ever hear the call of the wild trout?

I duck, look to the trailer for a second, the guy still blink blink blink.

Deke says, right out loud, Never? I thought you were smarter than that, kid. You got to be up on this stuff. Maybe I'll show you sometime. Probably not, though. Freak like you would tell everyone, blab it all over.

Deke goes by, back and forth, in front of my eyes, in a long blur as I shake my head.

Deke says, Well, we'll see.

I get up to pee, trying to calm down, and I end up walking down the driveway, right down to where the fence gate is open next to a big sign that says, Good Fishing! No license needed – no limit!

I walk back and Deke is quiet. We pull them in and lay them stunned in the cut grass. Deke glances at the trailer every few minutes.

Deke whispers, You ever think that these fish might have something wrong with them, kid?

I smile at Deke, wiggling.

Deke whispers, You ever eat raw fish, kid?

I waggle my head, smile because I know Deke is wondering about it.

Deke says, not so whispery, You know, them Arabs, they eat it all the time. Getting three squares out of raw fish. Crullers. You know they eat crullers? Right on the subway, straight out of the box. Raw fish and crullers!

I'm looking to the trailer, then to Deke.

Deke throws her head back, says, Hah! You've never seen anyone eat so much raw fish and crullers!

The trailer door flings open, bounces off the aluminum side, and then slams shut. It opens again with a man behind it, a shotgun in his hands, looking into the darkness, peering.

In a voice so quiet it could be from the water at our feet, Deke slowly says, All you got to do is not move.

My hands shake and my feet are flopping in the grass, and I try to picture myself in bed asleep, which makes it worse, so I picture dogs running after cars, which makes me want to start panting and barking. I picture dogs humping.

The man puts one hand up to shade his eyes, getting a better look, his head jerking around.

Deke whispers, Just. Don't. Move.

The man bangs back inside and then bangs back out, this time coming down the steps and stopping. The square of light behind him blurs his outline.

I try to make movements that are invisible, imagined movements that take away some of the pressure. I drive off a cliff. I ride a bike that makes all the vacuum cleaners in town go at once. I rip out wires with my bare hands.

The man is slightly turned from us, facing the other pond when he says, When I catch you I'm going to cut you up and make you trout food.

He waits a few seconds, then says, I mean it.

He shakes his fist and goes back inside.

Deke leans back in the grass, starts pulling in a trout.

Deke says, Can you believe that? Guy used to be a teacher, used to be trusted by the parents of this town with their children. Now he wants to cut people up. But I don't think you should believe him. Guy's full of shit, kid. You hear his voice? A liar, no two ways about it.

Several fish later, Deke is telling me she can't believe how well trout can see at night when a pair of headlights ghost the fields and float toward us on the sound of an engine. Deke is sitting up. I see her moon face in the dim cast of the headlights. In the trailer door, a pushed aside curtain is replaced by a hand and face against glass.

Deke says, I knew it.

I pull Deke's shirt. The light gets brighter, and Deke is staring, and she says, I knew it, I just knew it.

I hit the deck in a place where I expect Deke not to hit the deck on me, and after hearing nothing I look up to see the lights brighter and Deke still sitting up, but the beams and engine noise go right past, then the red lights, some exhaust. The headlights hold on the trailer for a moment, then go off. A woman I see from church gets out. I see her long hair in the inside lit car as she leans back in to get something, and she walks to the door, knocks lightly, steps into a square of light that disappears with the shutting of the door.

Deke rebaits, casts out, sighs heavy. I can barely see her after all that light.

Deke says, Go home kid. Take my fish. See you tomorrow.

I don't move, wondering how invisible I am.

Deke says, Beat it.

I wrap my fish and walk away, crawl through the fence, head through the fields and woods to town.

At the Wheelers' I sneak into the dog pen in back and roll around with their two dogs, kicking, biting, snorting. When I leave they push the two fish I give them around in the dirt and grass with their noses, taking careful bites as if they're alive, and then ripping into them. The Wolfsons' dog knows it's me, rolls on his back, kicks his feet, makes these little arr-arr-arrRRrRr noises in his throat. I visit all the dogs in town and none of them bark and I feed them all. The only dog I don't see is the Browns', who is probably inside. When it starts getting light, I just throw the last fish into their yard and run home, climb the rose prickered trellis, squeak across the asphalt gripping roof, fly through my window onto my bed and into a fish fingered sleep.

Deke says, No more fishing, kid. Too dangerous.

So we fix vacuums, clean the innards of toasters and blenders, the sympathy work, Deke calls it, from the older women in town who used to come to her sermons, and at the end of the day we sweep up the dust, the dust from the skin of people we know here in town, the dust of me and Deke.

We don't talk much about fishing for awhile, and then Deke gets the stuff she ordered in the mail, the stuff she said would improve our night fishing. Out of the box she pulls some nighttime camouflage pants and a shirt, then those binoculars that you strap to your head, which Deke holds up like they're pretty nice, and she says they work by starlight, make everything at night visible.

Deke says to catch trout you've got to not only think like a trout, something everyone knows, but you've got to see like a trout, something only she knows, and now me. She puts the fisheyed goggles and the camo on in the shop when we're supposed to be fixing Mrs. Weather's wet vac. Deke moves around the tables and shelves like she's invisible, like a shadow at night, when she stands still she almost looks like a fish, body a certain color, specks on the fabric, and those goggle eyes. But she jerks her head in one direction and then in another, more like a chicken, as if something she's seeing isn't quite matching up to what she thinks is there. Deke leaps behind the oil drum trashcan, then peeks her head around the side, then back, then over the top, then takes giant quiet trout steps toward the phone on the wall, then suddenly, as if headlights have just passed over her body, she darts for the cover of a metal shelf and hits her forehead on the body of an ancient vacuum sticking out. Deke goes down on her back, starts flopping like a fish, arms over her forehead, going, Owowowowow, and I run to the sink to fill a bucket and dump it on her, then run out to the backyard to roll from one side to the other in the grass and dirt, making bug noises until I'm out of breath.

Deke says this town is full of holes. She says we think it's big enough for us to do what we want when we don't see eye to eye with someone. Deke says when we get in trouble we try to hide in those holes, like trout when they get spooked.

That afternoon, before we leave, Deke's got all new wires put in Mrs. Maxwell's vacuum, little snakes of yellow, red, green, and black. She smiles at her work, but she looks exhausted. Her cheeks, which used to be tan, are now going pale and saggy, and we're getting behind. Her hands are big and white, and the gold ring looks ready to cut right through.

Deke says that night we went out she caught five more trout and ate them all when she got home, says they weren't so great, not like wild trout.

Deke says, Fried them in a pan anyway, lots of butter. You learn that in the Marines. You can fry anything in a pan. Melt some butter, melt some more butter. Put the trout in, four minutes a side, salt, whatever. More butter on top, you're eating.

I pick up the goggles and feel the zings going up and down my arm and I look at Deke. She watches me and I can see her thinking on something.

Deke says, What we need is a new plan.

Wiggle, wiggle.

Deke says, Here's ten bucks. Go get us some fuel, something from the deli, and some cokes, we need a plan.

On the way and back, running, I think trout thoughts to get ready and when we're eating Deke says, I've got a plan I think might work, might just catch us more fish than you could believe. What do you say, kid? You want to go fishing again?

Zingggg! Pop! Pop! Zip-zip-zip-bing! Reee!

I'm crouching by the windowsill. In the thin light from the streetlight I see all the things in my room that I can't break. The bed with an iron frame, the heavy oak desk for schoolwork, the heavy oak chair, the heavy oak bureau. I remember the broken mirror, lamp, wind chimes, framed pictures, action pieces, Revolutionary war figures, the baseball card collection that I chewed up thinking about something else.

The street lights go off. I don't move, see how long I can stay still. My whole body is a place where dogs run at high speeds, so fast they begin to glow, bouncing off the inside walls, gaining speed until they're a blur of lights like snakes of electrical wires, free of dust, the wires carrying electricity at incredible speeds, and my head begins to shake out of control. The whole room is vibrating so fast that it goes blurry, and I bite down on the windowsill to try to keep things still. Deke says I shouldn't do this, she sees me do it sometimes. She says I'm just making it worse on myself, so I do it alone when no one can see me at my worst.

I don't remember the sneaker grabbing asphalt roof or the rosebush whispering trellis I'm down them so fast. Past the shop where I can see a new pizza box on the trashcan where it won't fit, then through the woods, into fields, saying a Hey cow hey cow warning. More woods and then the field with the fence and Deke, who told me she had to come early to keep an eye on things, but when I get there she's sitting with her back to the fence, her starlight goggles on, eating a meatball sub. I sit next to her, lean my back against the fence. Her head sometimes turns to look over the field, across the ponds, beyond where the drive leads past the open gate and eventually into town. I look and I know I can't see what Deke sees. Deke eats and goes back to staring at the trailer with the one light on, the man walking back and forth, making the light blink. I open one eye and keep the other eye shut, then open the shut eye and close the open one, back and forth.

Deke finishes her sandwich, crumples up the wrapper in her huge hands and stuffs it in her pack. She wipes her hands on her can't see in the dark camo pants, then burps a few times quick into her fist.

Deke says, You know what I wish? I wish I could just pull on a rope and have the sun come up.

We sit quiet for awhile.

Then Deke turns, grabs my shirt, and she says, Now look, I'm only going to tell you this once, so get it straight the first time. When no one's around, no one that's looking to kill them, the trout have a certain call they make. Sort of lets everyone know that all is clear. You know, start eating, that kind of thing. This making any sense?

I'm nodding so fast that my neck goes crack crack crack.

Deke says, So the idea is to make the call of the wild trout first, and you've got to make it right. Don't and you're fucked.

Deke is silent for a moment, and I don't know why but I start nodding like mad.

Deke says, Cut that shit out. Now listen to me, listen to the noise I make. You ready? Here it is. Aaaarrp!

I shrink back for a second her voice is so loud.

Deke says, Okay, now you do it.

I go, Aaaarrph!

Deke goes, No, not ph! AaaarrP! P!

I can hear in Deke's voice her need for me to say it right.

Deke says, Aaaarrp!

I go, Aaaarrp!

Deke says, That's it! Now, listen.

Deke grabs the front of my shirt, her hand so fast in the dark. Rocket engines, fuses burning.

Deke says, This is nothing to fuck around with. You don't tell anyone what the call of the wild trout is. You understand me?

She lets go of my shirt and starts walking. I figure she's going to the place we usually go, but she veers off and brings us right up to the trailer, me squinting and Deke raising the goggles to her forehead. Her face shines with sweat and her mouth hangs open. She doesn't look very good. I can see Mr. Leeder clearly, walking up and back in the living room. Looking at the floor, his mouth moving like he's saying something.

Deke motions her head toward the ponds and we set up our lines.

Deke catches something almost immediately and I'm all tensed for that lightning bolt to come through my fingertips. Deke reels in and says, Nothing like doing some fishing, eh boy?

She whacks the fish on the head with her knife handle, the hollow thock thock thock.

I'm nodding like there's no tomorrow.

Deke says out loud, Yep. Sit back, catch a few trout, talk about old times. That's the way!

The zings go up and down my back, splinter out to my skin. I look to the trailer and there's nothing except the shape of Mr. Leeder moving back and forth.

Then Deke decides to be quiet, just us reeling in trout, Deke whacking them, laying them on the grass, until the headlights come and Deke is standing up, the lights passing for a moment right over her then me with my face in the ground, my arms out flat, biting onto some grass.

Mr. Leeder comes out, opens the car door, looks into the darkness as the lady I see from church gets out with her long hair in the light, him standing like he knows there's something out there. Then they go inside, the lights go off.

Deke sighs and it sounds like all the air is leaving her.

Deke says, The thing about fishing is that no matter how many you get, you never feel like you're getting enough.

She starts digging around in her bag.

Deke says, You ever hear of M80s?

Deke strikes a match, lights a smooth stick on fire, throws it into the water.

Deke says, You've go to coat the wick with wax.

The water goes Mooommmph!

The ground gives a quick shake and I hear the water start to boil.

Deke is on her knees, peering out over the pond, then saying, Okay, here they come.

Deke walks into the water, starts picking up white-bellied fish, putting them in her creel.

The door of the trailer swings to slam open, shoeless and shirtless Mr. Leeder runs just past the woman's car, holding a shotgun in his hands.

He says, I know who you are.

I'm in a ball, curled as tight as I can to bring in my knees and elbows, my head trying to get in the space between my knees and my chest, my feet curled in, my toes curled in.

I hear the slam of the shotgun and look up to see her in the water all the way up to her neck, just her goggled head sticking out, then I look to see him looking toward the other pond.

He says, I hear you in them bushes!

He raises the shotgun again and shoots into the trees across the pond, the flash of the gun lighting up the surface like an eye blinking. I'm about to scream, I'm shaking my head around to throw the sounds from one side to the other, to keep them in, to keep them from landing and boring a hole right through my head.

He says, You're no match.

Then he laughs, or makes a laughing noise, and goes back inside.

Deke moves toward me, says, Meet me by the fence in two minutes.

She grabs something from her pack and is gone.

Suddenly there's too much to do at once. I look at my shirt full of fish, Deke's pack, my pack, our lines, the bobbers, and it's too much to know what to do first. I throw my line to the ground and flop like a fish, wriggling and flapping. Then I get up and throw myself to the ground, then I do it again, thinking fish thoughts, capture, suffocation.

I reel in the lines, stuff everything into Deke's bag, including my shirt full of fish, and hunchback my way to the fence, where I look back to see a quick spark near the trailer, and then I hear the call of the wild trout getting louder, getting closer.

Then one of Deke's trout bombs goes off down by the trailer. Deke lets out a laugh, she goes right by me, making all sorts of laughing and panting breathing noises, the trailer light comes on, the figure runs out the door, coming straight for me.

I give it a few seconds, just thinking about this man running my way with a gun, and then I'm off, running so fast I picture myself a blur, and I blow right by Deke who is stopped, bent over, hands on knees, breathing like a panting dog, and I leave her there. She says wait up but I don't.

The Wheelers' dog rolls and rolls, grunts and shakes, licks my ears until I'm rolling and tingling and laughing, me licking back, our tongues licking each other. The Williams' pair sniff and we lie down for a short while in the dirt at the end of the yard. The Browns' dog is inside, pawing the glass door to the backyard, sniffing at the edges. The Maxwells' dog tries to climb on top and I bite her quick on the shoulder, then we lie together and clean each other until I fall asleep, her muzzle under my chin.

She doesn't ask about me, but I know she's doing something. Deke and I don't say much during the days, we don't do much, her thinking's somewhere else completely, and then one morning

I get to the shop to find Deke with a cut on her elbow and a swollen nose that looks like it might have been bleeding.

Deke says, Never mind, kid, because I ain't gonna tell you. Besides, you don't look so good yourself. Your eyes are all droopy, and you smell like a kennel.

Deke doesn't look good, and she's sitting on her stool, eating doughnuts that don't seem to please her. She stops mid chew and looks at me.

Deke says, Why don't you go home for the day, just take the day off.

She waves her hand, perfectly normal, get lost. She does this about every other day.

I start sweeping.

The bell at the front door rings, and Deke jumps to a crouching position, eyes staring at the door to the front of the shop. She whispers, Who the fuck do you suppose that is?

I see her eyes are red rimmed, worn.

I find Mrs. Weeder, come to pick up her machine, unfixed, which I give her, go to the back to find Deke sitting on the floor, eating a doughnut like she just can't help it anymore.

Deke looks up at me, says, You still here? Thought I told you to go home.

I ask Deke about fishing and she says no way but I can smell it on her, the way you smell it on a dog that keeps going back to something dead in the woods.

A few days later Deke's got a black eye and she won't say where it's from. She puts away a bag of potato chips, then a bag of pretzels, and four cokes, which she drinks by holding the can in her hand and swaying her shoulders back as if there's something wrong with her arm.

She looks at me and says, Kid, you don't look so good. You ought to get out of the house more often.

Her skin is pale and puffy around her knuckles and wrists, under her chin, the waist of her pants looking like they pinch, her shoelaces untied. She finishes a coke and cracks open another one. She stares at a pile of tangled wiring in front of her, her eye circled in blacks and yellows and purples, a cut on her lip I didn't notice before, scratches on her hands, dirt under her fingernails.

Deke says, Just look at you. Dark circles under your eyes. Skinny as a fucking stick, you got grass stains everywhere. It looks like you haven't brushed your teeth in about a year. Christ, kid, you better get to work on yourself.

The shop is a mess. There are orders that were supposed to be done last week, two weeks ago, the shelves are full, the trash cans are full, the floor is covered with wires and dirt and balls of dust.

Nobody has mentioned fishing, but Deke shakes her head, says, That's it. No more fishing.

She leans on the door frame to the back room, her face haggard, half a forgotten muffin in her hand, her mouth open as if she's out of breath.

I know she'll give in.

At night I roll with the dogs in town and wonder what Deke is doing.

More people start coming in to get their vacuums and blenders and toasters back, the ones that haven't moved since we put them on the shelf.

At some point Deke stops paying me.

The shelves are starting to empty.

Deke says, Look around you, kid. How you ever seen so much light? You'll never be able to remember this.

I let Deke catch me reading one of her magazines and a few hours later, Deke says, That's it. All we need is more light, and the way to get more light is to make more light. Maybe you can help me with this one. You want to help?

Wag, bong! Bong!

Deke says, Okay, kid. Tonight. Leave your fishing stuff at home. We're going to catch them in the light.

I'm out the window, down the trellis, pack thrown to the ground so I don't crush the cookies with my rolling across the lawn like dust rolled together in a strong wind, the wind changing, me the dust boy rolling back.

The smell of gasoline is more powerful than the pastrami and mustard, the pumpkin pie, the beer.

Deke says, I got two cans but they're five gallons apiece, so we'll only have to make one trip. I think it'll be enough. I don't want any shadows at all.

Deke is being kind of nice, giving me sips of her beer, moving around like her body is hers and not something someone just gave her.

Deke says, Okay, freak boy. Lock and load.

My head waggles and my toes are tapping out of control.

The cans are heavy and I picture bullet nosed jets and lightning bolts and then as fast as I can I go about fifty feet, thinking of tanks. Deke can carry hers pretty well but she starts sweating right away and opening her mouth to breathe. We have to lie down once in the cow field, just lie on our backs and let the sparks fade from our vision, the heavy and almost painful throb in our chests and throats.

Deke says, Kid, you ever have sex?

I'm up and running in circles, my arms hanging down, bouncing and jerking wherever they want to go, my mouth going, Buh-buh-buh-buh… and the sparkles come back and I dive bomb to the grass next to Deke, out of breath again.

Deke says, Well, when you do, remember to think to yourself, Here I am. I'm right here with this person I love, and this is what I'm doing. Say to yourself, Later, I'm going to remember this and I'll know it was true and right now here I am, I'll always have this. Remember to do that, kid, next time you're screwing.

She rolls over to me, puts her hand on my chin, turns my face to her.

I know Deke is doing the wrong thing.

Deke smiles, says, Okay, soldier. Not much more to go.

At the fence I think I have turned into an ape. I can feel the tingles going up and down my arms, and the ends of my fingers feel like they're dragging in the grass.

Deke leans on the fence, panting, says, Okay, downhill.

We both see that the trailer light is already off, the woman's car already there.

We drag the cans downhill and Deke is suddenly alive. She opens the first can, then in a slow walking crouch, she starts moving around the edge of the pond, sloshing gas out of the can. As soon as I see what she's doing I grab the other can, start to picture a dog running around a big circle, start dragging the can to the other pond, and Deke stands up, points at me, and barks, Put that down.

I jump to the ground, hide it in the grass.

Deke times it so she makes it around once and is out of gas.

I scurry to roll under the trailer and I can look out and see Deke moving, and I can hear the two dogs above me, making rolling in the dirt noses, grunting and pushing and other sounds.

She takes the other can, slow walk crouches around the pond, dribbling gas around once until the can is empty.

The air is heavy with gasoline. I smell it heavy on Deke when she waves me over, grabs my shoulder, says, Wake up kid. This is no time to sleep. This is a time to be awake. This is a time to remember.

Deke's voice is moving all over the place, going up and down, making little noises between the words I've never heard her make.

Deke sits down in the grass to look at the ponds, and I go back to my den and after awhile the dogs rolling around noises above me stop, and sometime later Deke stands up, I see her arms move, then a tiny spark arcs out over the water and before it hits the surface and orange flame spreads out, fingers along the weeds at the edge, and creeping inward, turning more blue toward the center.

Deke has lit the second pond and it is moments behind in completing the circle, moving in toward the center, and then the sound starts, coming from Deke. The rising trout call that is slower, louder, coming from somewhere deep inside her.

Now the flames have grown to two circles of orange fire lighting up the darkness of the field like eyes coming up from beneath the ground.

I watch for a moment more, and then I'm gone, not turning to the sounds behind me. I go to the Wheelers' house and let their dog go, then to the Lincolns' house, then to the Smiths' house, the Dwyers' house, the Woollys' house, the Weeders' house, and they all follow me through the streets, running wild and chasing each other, through the side yards, across the little league field, humping, eating grass, knocking over garbage cans, chasing cats, to the Browns' dog and I let us into their yard.

We roll and grunt and snort and run run run run.

Toward day, I put my hand on their backs to calm them down. I place the empty water dish on my head and they fall in around me.

TOR *Ulven*

The Sea

A tug. Then motionless. Then a little trembling. Then motionless. A new tug, then motionless, a little trembling, and so on, red, gracile, like a limb on some exotic insect, a tentacle perhaps.

Sometimes I try just looking. Or just hearing. Oddly enough it works to remember something with your eyes open, covering your ears, and you can see something you once did, and hear something you once heard, at the same time that you see the room you are sitting in, and hear for example the sound of a warbler or a jet or both, you see memories, as if you had your eye turned inward (with an attached organic lantern, like a deep-sea fish), a view into your brain, where the memories lay stored, in a torpor, a throng of strange animals; some are slow and sluggish, cold, poikilothermic, they move unwilling and heavy, while others have appeared so often that their fur has become matted and disheveled, but the worst is that many are some kind of night animal, or underground animal, meaning that one can barely see an ear or the tip of a tail disappearing, and even more of them, presumably most of them, one never sees at all.

A chain of cockleshells, matte gray-white, with varying brown stripes across their flutes, which radiate and spread out in a fan shape from the nozzle-like foot section (where the open-and-close muscle once sat).

They are there, but they never show themselves. All of these invisible memory animals (like bacteria and the other necessary or unnecessary parasites in my own body) will die when I die, and that will again mean that not just that which one knows, knows as oneself, will disappear, but also that that which one does not know and perceive, does not know as oneself, which one has never known anything about, will also disappear, forever, without anyone ever having the possibility of learning to know the unknown. That which no one will ever be able to know anything about interests me. Not because it is a secret. I cannot stand secrecy. I say everything as it is. The most obvious is the most incomprehensible. Let us say that I decided on a day, a date, a year, a day I have absolutely no memory of, and I decide now and know that the memory of that day, minute by minute, exists someplace, but it is impossible to recall again, as if it was a priceless collectible, and it had been stolen and sold to an unknown and untraceable collector who now has incorporated this day into his collection of days, or as if someone (who knows who) has placed it in a jar, and sealed the jar, and placed it down in a crypt, or a hole, with a lid on, and not just that day but every single day I have forgotten, in its own jar, a whole line of sealed-up jars, down in a crypt, or a hole, and he (who knows who) who knows where the crypt or the hole is is gone, and the line of sealed-up jars which contain my forgotten days sit there and will never be opened again. But there is no thief and no collector, no sealed-up jars in their crypt or hole, it is a day I myself have lived, and which like any of my living days before it is not just gone, but whose trace is even gone.

About a half dozen tiny conches with, along their length, brown and blue-black stripes in clearly defined tirelike fields which are seen slightly twisted in relation to each other so that the lines, so to speak, are out of phase and, becoming smaller, change into dots before they disappear completely at the white tip.

To return, I do not remember which day, which date, and which year it was when with a kiss it happened. It was that day in my youth when I walked home from a party, or better said, from a house where there had been a party, walked because I could not afford a cab, and the last bus had long since gone. It was in the middle of winter and very cold, though I kept somewhat warm by walking fast. It took hours. I do not remember so much of the actual walk, except that the gravel crunched when I walked through the pedestrian subway, and that there stood icy trees on a slope. The wind had blown the snow into sort of roils or waves around them, so one could imagine the trees plowing through white-whipped froth like masts of God knows what sinking ship, presumably a ship with a deck of frozen ground, a hull of earth, and a cargo of stone, and now the sails were reefed, but in the summer the ever-sinking ship would have full-blown sails of leaves.

A palmlike scallop shell, mother-of-pearl white glimmering on the glistening outside, but inside with a reddish sandstone-colored coarse surface which in the hollows becomes microscopic, porous, and very rough lamellas across the shell's laths, which in turn lay fluted like Greek temple columns, though they thin and flatten out to nothing at the base, as if they pointed back to the formless point they once sprang from.

It is like thoughts one can comfort oneself with on meaningless wanderings in winter, when one's face becomes stiff, one's hands and toes numb, while one's thoughts continue to keep themselves warm. In certain situations a warm brain is more important than a warm heart. The reason I remember this is because one of the girls at the party, completely unexpectedly, gave me a kiss on the cheek in parting, and though she was not especially pretty or charming, an unexpected kiss (even on the cheek) is still something one remembers, at any rate if one has gotten (and given) as few kisses as I have, considering my age, despite everything, and because bodily contact from the other sex at that time was not as strongly devalued as it is now, and because the kiss represented a pleasure out of the ordinary. A beautiful pleasure. More objectively considered, it left a trace of moisture on my cheek, which later chilled in the icy winter weather, something which, by the way, for one reason or another, makes this memory more dear. (I have since then gone over it so many times that I am almost not able to separate my recollection of the memory from the memory itself; it is like a statue of a saint which has been kissed so often that all trace of toenails and toes have disappeared – regarded theoretically, one can imagine that the adoration will in the end wear away the adored, which finally draws itself back to nothingness and remains there.) But now I have gone far from my original intent, which was to see. Suddenly one evening I discovered a blue light which had not been there before (it must have been some sort of advertisement), and I also did not know where the building was, since I have not always been to those areas I can see from the window here, not to mention having not been out of the house for nine years, six months, and twenty-four days. I still do not know where the building with the blue light stands, and even with binoculars it is impossible to read what the advertisement recommends. So it means something to others, but nothing to me.

When I for once had washed the floor, with a long broom, bucket, washcloth, and soapy water (it took the whole day), and when I had finally neared the dresser, with my back to it, the broomstick knocked the thing over, and it fell down.

However that may be, I now see, this very minute, somewhere behind that building, that is, at least a few kilometers as the crow flies, the black arm of a moving crane at work, a slanting line over the whitish sea and the gray-black islands which can be glimpsed back there, or rather, if I follow it long and hard, I can see how the black line first slopes to the left (for me) then changes to a straight somewhat shorter line and then becomes a black line which slopes to the right (for me) before the whole thing repeats itself in the opposite direction, and it comes to me now that what that crane lifts up (or down) belongs to the category of things I will never know anything about, I can only sit and watch it, just as a person can watch a distant planet and never know what it looks like, or one can watch a wild animal in a cage and never know what it is to be the animal yourself, or like I can watch the pebble on the dresser and never have the experience of being a stone, an experience basically no one, upon closer reflection, not even the stone itself, enjoys, since a stone has no mode of perception and therefore can have no experience of how it is to be a stone, it has no ego, so to speak, it is completely unselfish, it can only be seen from without and identified as a stone, a pebble; but upon closer reflection it is of course also the same for all vegetation, exactly the same for seaweed on a rotten oar as for a giant ancient oak on a hilltop, just as the poet's wish to be for example a tree in the woods is impossible to fulfill, for no one is a tree in the woods; to be a tree in the woods would basically be the same as being dead, or at any rate unconscious, in a coma without ever waking, the tree in the woods a coma without ever waking. O if I were but a coma in the woods, without ever waking.

Two small shells that are black on the outside, but inside have a gradient scale of color tones from deep ink-blue to white (closest to the pointed tip), aside from one of them having at the bottom remnants of very fine-grained gray-white sand, which (maybe on account of a long-dried secretion) sticks to the shell, where the sand lies in an ellipse, open on one side, reminiscent of a miniature lagoon.

If consciousness, and the human par excellence, can be thought of as noise, a sort of perpetual never-resting noise, then there exists as well in stones and plants a stillness which basically is inconceivable, a stillness which is even greater since it cannot be experienced by anyone. Upon closer reflection the same stillness which exists inside of us from the moment we again become lifeless matter, since no one can say: I am a bone, just as a stone or a patch of seaweed can never say: Ego sum.

A tug, then motionless, then a little trembling, then motionless, then a tug again, and so on, without going anywhere, the long red line hesitating over the short black line by the number (the lines by every number a little thicker than the others), without ever reaching the next line but also without the tugging ever stopping.

The elephant. If I now move my gaze from the moving crane far away there, and pull it into the room (as if two antennas extended from my eyes to reach whichever points I see fit to fix on, these antennas will contract, from a length of over two kilometers to about two meters), then my gaze meets the green elephant where it hangs from a loop extending from the top of its head, and softly turns from side to side, almost imperceptibly, from some indoor wind, if one can call it that. (It all seems to be about animals today.) It is mainly signal green, though it is becoming a truth with modifications to say that it is green, since it has through the years become covered with a layer of nicotine-infested dust, which in some places definitely gives the nylon hide a more brown than green color. It also has white in its ears, and has a sort of jersey on with wide horizontal stripes of red, orange, pink and gold (from top to bottom), and a bright red bow tie around its neck, and its eyes (or rather its eye – from my point of view one eye is hidden by the merry upturned trunk) are brown.

Three or four glossy snail shells which on one side end in a jagged opening, which resembles a slanting, grinning mouth.

It is certainly meant to be a source of comfort and encouragement for someone. For sentimental reasons, I guess, I am just not able to throw the elephant away, and it is much too infested with dirt and nicotine smell for me to be able to give it away. One ends up not getting rid of things because one has mucked them up too much. The elephant is moreover the only piece of fauna in the house, my house pet, so to speak, if one disregards all of the animals, and that is not a few, that I am able to conceive in my imagination, both truly living and imaginary (as for example memory animals). After this homecoming to things near, it is perhaps time to move out into the world again. With the eye, that is, only with the eye. (Sight is basically the most impotent of all the senses, it is the sense that reaches the farthest and possesses the least; if one hears music, for example, one possesses the sound in a way, and if one smells an orchid, for example, one possesses in a way the smell, and if one holds something in one's hand, an old bicycle or bread dough or an ax handle, then it is at any rate near, though one does not possess it; but one can only imagine how it would be if the eye could actually draw to it and own everything it could take in, it would be impossible to exhibit goods, the windows would be sucked empty of objects, but not only the windows, all the shops would have to completely cover things with blankets and tarps, and the customer would not be able to see a thing before it was paid for, but, upon closer reflection, everyone would have to keep their things hidden, or else it would lead to total breakdown of private property, and also of all collective property, every object would rotate continually among owners who saw them one after the other; but if the principle of the absolute ability of the gaze to possess would then be extended to concern also the so-called carnal desires, or for that matter aggressions, it would lead to such endless complications and confusions that every social life would be in practice impossible; here it is best to stop this line of thought.)

It fell into two pieces, and I tried to put it together again. It surprised me a little that the face of the clock was only a thin paper plate with a hole in the middle (for the hands). I could have placed it upside down or sideways had I wanted. I put it upright and fixed together the housing, which is made of white plastic, with tape. Afterward I discovered that it both worked and did not work at the same time.

I now let my gaze wander in an approximately straight line across the horizon, west from the black diagonal of the mobile crane, and it meets, after awhile, and at varying distances: a tree (tiny and indeterminate); a pale yellow towerlike building (which I know to be a transformer station); a clothes drying pole which can turn in the wind; the tiled roof of an apartment building with two chimney pipes and four ventilation pipes as well as a roof hatch; a large apple tree (so close I could hit it with a ball); a large but in the distance smaller building with many windows and balconies (which I know to be a hospital); a high-voltage tower; a chimney, from here seen to be the size of my little finger, but in reality closer to a hundred meters high, and equipped with a red warning light on the top (clearly visible at night), but I will presumably not fly out of this pipe after I have been cremated, though it belongs to the hospital, for it probably services the hospital's central heating system, and will therefore be used to keep warm those who are always warm, not to turn into smoke those who are cold.

Two blue mussel shells which are no longer blue on the outside, nor black, but on the contrary white, a partly matte, partly glossy whiteness full of scars and marks, that is to say, that part of the shell that is visible looks like that, but about half of both shells is completely overgrown with a bristly, beehivelike, and dried-up clump of something, which must be acorn barnacles or some similar small animal, dense, almost on top of each other, and which are made in turn of an egglike shell with an oval hole on top, and most of these shells are filled with something roundish, divided in the middle by a column, so that the whole thing reminds one of an old crone with a kerchief tucked carefully around her face. But if so, then a whole group of old crones with kerchiefs tucked carefully around their faces, a whole mass of people staring at the observer of those two one-time parasite-teased blue mussels, though all of these tiny shells are also empty, and are thus more like jars or vessels. (Perhaps one can imagine that it was here that some of my forgotten days once existed, like rolls of microfilm washed by the sea?)

It is basically typical. The chimney that I, turned into smoke, will one day fly out of, I cannot see. On the other hand, I would not, after all, be able to sit and watch, with a contented sigh, the smoke of myself fly out of some chimney anyway. But through the uneven spaces between the building, the drying pole, the trees, and so on I get a glimpse of the sea, certainly not blue, not even gray-blue, but white-gray like fog, as if it strictly taken could be something other than the sea, maybe clouds, in which case my eyes would be high mountain peaks which stuck up over the gray cloud layer, but I do not like tiring quarrels, so I say it right out: It is the sea that I see.

The battery is still working. But the hand mechanism has somehow been lodged tight, so that the electrical impulse which would otherwise keep the clock going only leads to tentacle-like tugs on the second hand.

After only having seen the sea at a distance of many kilometers over a period of nine and a half years, I have more or less forgotten the feeling of warm beach sand under my feet, forgotten the sound of the surf, forgotten how the beach at low tide with seaweed actually looks, forgotten how it feels to hold a jellyfish in my hand, forgotten the smell of the sea, the feeling of the sea, the vision of the sea.

A piece of seaweed, coal-black (aside from each light clinging grain of sand) and dried, embalmed in a weak elastic, but crisp bush-shaped, almost weightless in the hand, but if you put your nose right up to it, you can still smell the characteristic, actually indescribable fragrance of the sea.

The short hand points to five, the long hand to ten, the thin needle for the alarm to eight. The second hand to three, on the way to the next line, without ever making it there: a tug, then motionless, a trembling, a tug, and so on.

I no longer remember when or where the marine relics originated from, but certainly not from the summer I am now thinking of, and which I remember. That is to say, I remember only one episode, or something that scarcely merits the term episode, something that could have taken two or three seconds. By a strange circumstance I was on vacation by the sea with three women (although one of them was supposed to be my darling), and the weather was warm and nice, like the way I hear the weather was in the old days. We swam, the women put on two-piece bathing suits, and suddenly one of them said that she would have liked to forget about (here she said my name) and take off her top, if we (that is, the three women and I) had been alone, but we were not, and she did not take off her top. Nothing more than that. I occasionally get the feeling that I remember more things that did not happen, that never came of anything, than I remember incidents which unfolded in their full splendor. According to my dictionary (and I quote), *the intestine goes through the heart* of the mussel. It occurs to me that this bit of information could be used for something. The smell of the sea. My present sea exists in a blue plastic container about ten by twenty centimeters, with a see-through lid, and if there is something which characterizes these relics from the sea, it is a marked dryness. There is not a drop of water of the ocean which once surrounded them, or covered them, or moistened them with high tide, if nothing else. The lid has a large crack across it, and does not fit completely on top, since one of the shells is too high. The smell of the sea. The alarm clock which neither works nor does not work sits on top of the container, as if they belonged together, with the pebble as a silent witness to the side. I no longer look out toward the horizon, I no longer see the working crane or the chimney I will never fly out of,

I try just looking at the clock, at the red second hand, which continues to tug and tremble, indefatigable, without going anywhere, without being able to gallop around the minute-strewn circus ring. The station clock. Yes, I remember. It was green with a white face, and the second hand was black, an old-style clock with iron workings and wings with wheels on top, mounted at an angle to the wall of the waiting room. It was late one night. From the dance in the barn we took a cab in to the center of the little coastal town. The last train had gone. It was a side track without electricity. The driver asked Central on his radio if there was a night train from the junction station, and there was, and we drove fifty kilometers inland in the middle of the night. The car's headlights gliding over endless kilometers of empty and dark asphalt, there were almost no buildings, as if the woodlands lay deserted in waiting for unknown pioneers. The only living being we observed the whole trip was a badger or something like it which bounded across through the headlights' never-resting light, that is to say non-resting, I mean unmoving, then we reached the station and a handwritten piece of paper, fastened to the information board with a thumbtack, explaining that the night train was canceled. The waiting room was closed. The station house stood in the middle of the woods. There was not a single building for miles around. We sat on the green wooden bench until seven o'clock the next morning. When we finally got home we slept about twelve hours. It was of course a holiday. Once again vacation. She said I looked at you while you slept. You have deep lines on your cheeks; you did not have those before. For fear that she would not kiss me anymore, I had to blame my soul, that it had become more disillusioned and more cynical, I could not say that my teeth had rotted, especially not my molars. The more abstract sometimes has certain privileges over the concrete. I mean, it seems somehow more stylish to have a dilapidated soul than a dilapidated limb. Though a certain converted effect is also applicable; if one is just an ordinary cripple without any facility for speech worth mentioning, sitting like a ludicrous slobbering frozen dancer in a wheelchair, then it helps if one has an international capacity in, for example, malacology or theoretical astrophysics. Yes. The elephant man's eloquent conversation. Now I hear someone on the stairs. The limping step. It must be him. He goes up every stair steadying himself with a cane, which one, thanks to the rubber knob, almost does not hear. He has a fear of elevators, that is his only weakness, so he goes up the stairs instead. The person who wants to avoid him has to take the elevator up and down endlessly. Sleep on a cot in the elevator. Have food stuck lightning-quick through the elevator doors. Throw leftovers and dirty silverware lightning-quick out of the elevator. Relieve themselves in a chemical watercloset in the elevator. Empty the bucket lightning-quick out through the elevator doors. Never be able to look out of a window, only into a mirror. (After a hundred days with only a view of a mirror, even the most self-centered and vain will beg for a window.) To sit locked up for an undecided length of time in a prison which, instead of the prisoner, went restlessly up and down the whole time. Did I not receive a letter today, by the way, with a handwriting which seems familiar but which I could not place? Yes. It is lying unopened on the dresser in the entryway. I just might be able to put it in my jacket pocket if I hurry. I was ready. I knew he would come one of these days, but not that it would be today. One always tries to push such things from oneself, or before oneself, or behind, as if one went backward, staring into the past or down into the now, the now at the tips of one's shoes, back to back pushing against someone one knows is stronger, who has not even yet used his strength. One last time I can close my eyes and imagine that he is a distinguished *gentil'uomo* who is coming to pick me up in his gondola, to take me through the brilliantly lit, slowly crumbling canal city. The doorbell rings. I go now to open.

Translated from Norwegian by Krister Swartz

authors

7 Zafer Şenocak
was born in Ankara in 1961 and has lived in Germany since age nine. He has published six books of poetry and essays and has translated into German the poems of Yunus Emres, a 14th century Anatolian mystic. His work in this issue is excerpted from *Der Mann im Unterhemd*, due out this fall from Babel Verlag. He currently lives in Berlin.

20 Javier Marías
was born in 1951 in Madrid. His seventh and most recent novel was awarded the prestigious Rómulo Gallegos prize for Spanish-language literature this year. He has taught in the US and UK and is the translator of work by Conrad, Stevenson, and Hardy, among others. "When I Was Mortal" was originally published as "Cuando fui mortal" in the newspaper *El país*, summer 1993.

32 Jáchym Topol
was born in Prague in 1962. His first novel, *Sestra* (Atlantis, Brno, 1994), from which "Cellars" is an excerpt, won the Egon Hostovský prize as the best Czech book of 1994. Besides having poems from *Sestra* set to music by his younger brother Filip's band, Psí Vojáci, Topol himself was once singer and songwriter with the underground band Národní třída and continues to write lyrics for Načěva. Several of his poems appeared in *Trafika* 2.

46 Joaquim Manuel Magalhães
won last year's Portuguese Writers' Association Prize for Poetry for *A Poeira Levada pelo Vento* (Editorial Presença, Lisbon, 1993), which includes "Sloten." He currently works as a professor of English Literature at the University of Lisbon. "Sloten" is his first publication in English translation.

62 Terje Holtet Larsen
was born in 1963 in Oslo. Author of two novels and two collections of short stories, he also edited last year's *De beste norske norvellene*, a collection of Norwegian short stories. "Unfortunate Canoe Quotes" (from the anthology *nye linjer*, Aventura, Oslo, 1994) is his first work published in English translation.

74 Mira Magen
currently lives and works as a nurse in Jerusalem. Her first collection of stories was awarded the prize for best first book of 1994 by the Israeli government. "The Red Dress," taken from this book, is her first work published in English translation.

82 Stephan Eibel
was born in 1953 in Eisenerz, Austria, and now lives in Vienna. He is the author of six books of prose and poetry and is also a playwright. "Paint," his first work published in English, is an excerpt from his most recent novel *In Österreich weltbekannt* (Freibord, Vienna, 1992).

96 Tomaž Šalamun
was born in Zagreb in 1941 and grew up in Koper, on the Istrian coast. He is the author of twenty-five books of poems, and his work has been translated into several languages, including, in English: *The Selected Poems of Tomaž Šalamun* (Ecco, 1988) and *The Shepherd, The Hunter* (Pedernal, 1992). The poems in this issue are from his latest book, *Ambra* (Mihelać, 1995).

108 Aamer Hussein
was born in Karachi in 1955. A regular contributor to such publications as the *Times Literary Supplement*, he is also a translator of Urdu and a lecturer in the Department of South Asian Studies at the University of London. His first

collection of short stories, *Mirror to the Sun*, was published by Al-Saqi Books last year.

132 Benny Barabash
was born in Beersheba in 1951 and currently lives in Tel Aviv. In addition to seven film scripts and plays, he has written two novels. "My Mother's Side" is an excerpt from his most recent book (published by Hakibbutz Hameuchad/Simon, 1994) and is his first work published in English translation.

140 Do Kh.
was born in Vietnam in 1955, served briefly in the South's army during the war, moved to France in 1969, and now lives with his Lebanese-born Saudi wife and two children near Los Angeles, where he works in the food manufacturing industry. In addition to publishing three collections of short stories and two of poetry in Vietnamese, he has also made two documentary films. His story in this issue was originally published in Vietnamese in 1991 and is his first work published in English translation.

154 Joost Zwagerman
completed his debut novel, *De houdgreep*, in 1986 at the age of twenty-three. He has since published two volumes of poetry, a collection of essays, and two more novels – *Vals licht*, which was nominated for the 1992 AKO Literature Prize, and *De Buitenvrouw* (De Arbeiderspers, Amsterdam, 1994), from which his story in this issue, his first to appear in English translation, is an excerpt.

164 Pierre Martory
published his first novel, *Chebus ou La Beau Marriage*, in 1953, and soon after stopped seeking publication in France, though he has continued to write diligently. A bilingual book of poems, *The Landscape Is Behind the Door* (Sheep Meadow Press) was published in 1994. His first book of poems in French is scheduled to be published in France next year by Alyscamps Press. He currently lives in Paris, where, from 1961-1985 he worked as a reporter for *Paris-Match*.

170 Hong Ying
became well known in China as a member of the "post-Misty" poets in the 1980s and only recently began writing fiction. Her work has won a number of prizes in China, Taiwan, and also England, where she now lives. "The Dirty Finger on the Bottle Lid" is her first story published in English.

180 Bear Kirkpatrick
lives in Kittery, Maine, where he is at work on his first novel. His work has also appeared in *The Quarterly* and *The Alaska Quarterly Review*.

200 Tor Ulven
achieved a sort of cult status as a prose stylist in Norway before his untimely death this past May at the age of forty-two. "The Sea" is from his fifth and most recent book of prose, *Vente og ikke se* (Gyldendal, Oslo, 1994), and is his first work published in English translation.

translators

7 & 82 Nancy Isenson
is an assistant editor of *Trafika*. Her translation of Oskar Wiener's 1919 book *Im Prager Dunstkreis* will be published by Twisted Spoon next spring.

20 Esther Allen
is a contributing editor of *Trafika* and assistant editor of *Mandorla*, a bilingual literary review in Spanish and English. Her translations of poems by Camila de la Mora appeared in *Trafika* 3.

32 Alex Zucker
has lived in Prague since 1990, where he worked as an editor for the now-defunct newspaper *Prognosis*. Among his non-literary translations from Czech are a history of the Laurin & Klement auto factory and a biography of architect Bohuslav Fuchs.

46 Richard Zenith
is an associate editor of *Trafika*.

62 & 200 Krister Swartz
is an associate editor of *Trafika*.

74 Sondra Silverston
moved from New York to Israel in 1970. She has worked as an editor and an investigative journalist and is currently a full-time literary translator.

96 Christopher Merrill
is a poet and non-fiction writer. His most recent books are *Watch Fire* (White Pine Press, 1994) and *The Old Bridge: The Third Balkan War and the Age of Refugees* (Milkweed, 1995).

132 Dalya Bilu
moved to Jerusalem from her native South Africa in 1957 and began translating Hebrew literature into English shortly thereafter. She has received both the American National Jewish Book Award for Fiction and the translation prize of the Israeli Ministry of Education and Culture.

140 Phan Huy Duong
is translator and co-editor of a recent anthology of contemporary Vietnamese short stories in French translation. His translations with Nina McPherson of Do Phouc Tien and Tran Trung Chinh appear in *Trafika* 3.

140 Nina McPherson
worked for several years as a journalist in China and now lives in Paris, where she is a full-time translator from Vietnamese and French.

154 David Colmer
lives in a former Catholic boys' school in a Muslim neighborhood of Amsterdam, where he is a translator of both Dutch and German. His own stories have also been published in England and his native Australia.

164 John Ashbery
lives in New York City. His most recent collection of poems, *Can You Hear, Bird*, is forthcoming in November from Farrar, Straus, and Giroux in the US and Carnacet in the UK.

170 Jenny Putin
was born in 1963 and received her PhD in Chinese literature from Oxford in 1992. She currently works for the Swansea Literature Festival.

Photo, Emmanuel Ortiz, the Old Bridge, Mostar

the globe
Bookstore and Coffeehouse
Open Daily
from 10:00 a.m.
until midnight
in libris, veritas;
in kava, vita
Janovského 14
170 00 Prague 7
e-mail: globe@ecn.gn.apc.org

***Trafika* wishes to thank the people and organizations listed below for their generous support, without which the production of this magazine would not have been possible.**

Friends
Benoit D'Aboville
John Allison
Zdenek Bakala
Thomas Baker
Erik Best
Jiři Brabec
Antonin Brandejs
James E. Burton
Anthony Caine
Hana Chandler
M. B. Christie
Michel Dooms
Robert Fishburn
Ivan Gabal
Michael Gold
Antony J. de V. Hill
Justin Hochberg
Katia Kastner
Neil King & Shailagh Murray
Nicholas Kirk
Peter Koch
Kevin Lansing
Mr. & Mrs. William J. Lemon
William Lobkowitz
Peter Magurean
Zach P. Messitte
Robert Mickey
Sam Orr
Ricardo Pau-Llosa
Mr. & Mrs. William Poff
Abel Parentini Posse
Stephanie Rosenfeld
Richard Saltzmann
William Sapers
John Seidler
Cathy & George Shriver
Marjorie Shultz
Marco Sipione
Magdalena Souček
Laurie Spengler
John Steinhilber
Lida Urbanek
Stephen Allan Vaughn
Alfons Vasiček
Jeff Walker
Stewart Wallace & Gabrielle Larew
J.M. Weiss
Betty Williamson
Richard & Helen Wood

Donors
Lillian Bell
Stephen Heintz
Jan & Jana Janků
Jeff & Jeanne Schwartz

Sponsors
Robert, Crystal, & Tim Benbow
John & Mildred Boyce
Thomas Porter

Patrons
Lauren Hook
Anna Lawson
Jeffrey Lee
Francesco Olivieri
John Bruce Shoemaker
The Council of Literary Magazines & Presses
The Mobil Foundation

Benefactors
Barbara Dickinson
The Fund for Central and East European Book Projects
The Open Society Fund – Prague
The Gulbenkian Foundation
The Berkowitz Family Foundation

Special thanks to
Suzy Basinger
Tom Brokaw
Patrick Cepr
Communication I Design
Foundation for the Production & Translation of Dutch Literature
Nina Gardner
Robert S. Glenn, Jr.
David Gross
Julia Hänsel
Institute for EastWest Studies
Anna Kareninová
Marta Miklušáková
Mimetic*
Susan Perry
George Plimpton
Will Rust